T Bar M Coach

T Bar M Coach

Richard "Leroy" Wines

T Bar M Coach

www.richardwines.com

To: Johnny Polk

Introduction

I've come to believe that there are three things that matter in life: people, experience, and faith. I've yet to encounter a place that has more of all three than T Bar M.

Every event in this narrative is true to the best that my imperfect memory recalls them. Memories grow fuzzy at the edges and many have passed to legend in my subconscious. This project is an effort to catch them before they are gone forever.

Names are hard. Rather than using the generic *coach*, I used real names of people present during the three summers I worked from 1994-1996. Many of the actions in these stories may have been performed by others than those named. If you are one of these, or if I have your name spelled wrong, I apologize. In most cases I used first names to keep the errors at a minimum. Let me know any errors and I'll be glad to change them in the next edit.

Thanks for being a part of this story—the story of my life.

Chapter One

The Choosing

A sign tacked on the dorm bulletin board catches my eye: *Ready for adventure?*

I can't help myself. I stop.

Tired of the same old boring summer job? Work at camp this summer. Over fifty camps interviewing at the Memorial Student Center. Tuesday, March 3rd, 10-4.

Today's Tuesday. I look at my watch. 3:20.

I think about summer school, my groundskeeper job at the intermural sports fields, and working for my dad building houses. I don't know anything about summer camp. Sure I went to church camp a couple of times in high school, but these are real camps. I've been in class since 8:00. Do I really feel like going over to the MSC? I shrug off the idea and head to my dorm room on the second floor. I'm too late anyway.

Halfway up the stairs, a voice like a breath of wind speaks into the back of my mind. *Go.*

But I don't really want to go. A nap would be so nice right now. *Go.*

I jog up the remaining steps to my room, do a quick underarm and face wash in the sink, and throw on a clean shirt with a collar. It's 3:25.

The lady at the reception desk of the MSC looks at me sideways. "Can I help you?"

I'm breathing hard. It's half a mile from my dorm to the MSC, and I ran. I wipe a bead of sweat from my brow. "Is there a—a summer camp job interview fair in here?"

She raises her eyebrows and then hands me a booklet. "Down the hall."

"Thanks." I scan through the booklet. It's filled with pictures of outdoor activities and good-looking college students beside names like Sky Ranch and Pine Cove with a brief description of the camp and the positions needed.

People sit along the wide hall behind tables with banners depicting kids and college age students fishing, riding horses, swimming, and smiling like they are having the best time of their lives. I walk past them all. It seems like there are hundreds. I look at my watch. 3:35.

One of the camps, Camp Olympia, catches my attention. I didn't realize they had camps focused on sports. I love sports, and I'm decent at volleyball and tennis. There's also this other camp with a strange name, T Bar M, that calls itself a "sports camp." I look up the Camp Olympia booth in the booklet, take note of its location, and head that way.

An older man and a college-aged girl sit facing each other behind the Camp Olympia sign and a table filled with colorful pictures and booklets.

I pick up a booklet and look it over.

A lady walks up with a bag of chips and a diet coke. "Interested in Olympia?" She moves behind the table and sits in a chair facing me.

The place looks cool enough. "I think so".

"Well, we've got one interview slot left, at 3:45." She looks down at her watch. "In five minutes."

I nod. "I'll take it." I give her my name and she writes it at the bottom of a piece of paper under at least twenty others.

Down the hall, many of the other camp booths are taking down their banners and packing things up. I look at the booklet. T Bar M should be about five booths down. Probably too late, but I walk down there anyway.

A clean cut man in a T Bar M polo shirt sits in front of a banner that reads *Christ Centered Adventure*. He's leaning back back in a chair with his feet propped up on the table in front of him.

Another guy, a little older and thicker than the first, stacks up brochures and puts them into a shoebox.

I stop. They're probably done for today. One interview should be enough anyway, and I'm lucky to even get that coming so late. I turn to go back.

"Looking to make an impact this summer?" the clean cut man asks.

I hesitate and turn to meet his eyes.

He lowers his feet to the floor and leans forward. His eyes glow with intensity or mental instability, I can't tell which. "You got a lot of camps in here, but there's only one that's the best, baby, this one! We got the most mind blowin' adventurin' moving back and forth you've ever seen. We got the ropes course screamer, the hillbilly holler, the fired up and goin' nuts every minute, Christ centered adventure, like nothing else." He slaps the table with his hand and stands up. He points to his jaw. "My name's jaw." He points to his knee, "knee." He pauses, grins, and pokes the other guy in the ribs, "poke."

The older guy drops some of the brochures. "Watch it!"

I think it's safe to assume that the glow in his eyes is mental instability. I look around to see if anyone is watching. Fortunately traffic is low at this time of day.

"I got time for one more interview," the guy, who I think is named Johnny, says. "What do you say? Ready for adventure?"

He's got to be crazy, but my heart skips at the sound of adventure. I'm not sure about all this. I've got the interview with Olympia—I glance at my watch—in one minute.

"I got an interview with Camp Olympia at 3:45." I look up and meet Johnny's eyes. My heart quickens and I get a feeling like a puzzle piece is snapping into place. I can't believe I'm considering this. "Could we maybe talk—after that?"

Johnny smiles. "I know James." He walks around the table and slaps me on the back. "We can interview you together." He heads down the hall toward the Olympia booth, his walk decisive and confident. He doesn't look back to see if I follow.

What is the Camp Olympia guy going to think about this? I hope he doesn't think I lined this up.

Johnny's already talking to the Camp Olympia guy when I get there. Does he even take a breath between sentences? "...and that way we can both get on the road before too late."

The Camp Olympia guy nods. There's not a lot he can say. He's small and compact, probably twenty years older than Johnny. He turns to me and sticks out a hand. "James."

"Richie."

"Why don't we take a seat?" James motions to the chairs where he had been talking to the girl earlier. He pulls up another chair and Johnny sits beside him.

James asks all the questions. He asks about my major, hometown, sports I play, and work experience. He writes my answers down on a notepad.

Johnny leans back during all this, quiet with a devious grin on his face. He doesn't even have anything to write on. I wonder if I should look at him or James when I'm speaking, and try to address both, but it feels awkward.

After about ten minutes of questions, James turns to Johnny. "Do you have any questions for Richie?"

Johnny smiles and leans forward. "Just one thing. If you were to die tonight and stand before God and He asked you, 'Why should I let you into My heaven?' what would you say?"

My heart beats faster. I know the answer, but I want to make sure I phrase it right. I take a deep breath. "There is no reason to let me in but grace. I believed in Your Son Jesus and have trusted Him to forgive my sins."

Johnny bolts up out of his chair, thrusts his arms over his head and shouts. "Going, Going, Gone! Homerun!" He whoops and holds his hand out for a high five.

This has to be the craziest guy I've ever met. I stand up and give him a weak high five.

People up and down the hall are looking at us.

I'd like to crawl under the table and hide, but the part of me awakened by that pinned up sign thirty minutes ago surges to life and I don't care. The familiar voice, like a hurricane wind now, blows toward the man standing before me. My choice has been made. I sit down. I can no longer stand.

Johnny sits back down. "That's all I need to know." He winks at me.

James rolls his eyes and gives me a hopeful look, but there is resignation there. He knows he's lost me. I will work at T Bar M.

Chapter Two

Arriving

The temperature gauge on "Old Gray," my 66' Chevy truck, creeps from yellow toward red. Would it be too much to ask for it to make one trip without something going wrong? Traffic on IH35 has been stop and go and my patched-up radiator can't keep up when the temperature goes above eighty-five and the driving speed below thirty. At least I'm over half-way there. I figured it'd take about three hours from Leroy to New Braunfels, so I gave myself four. With traffic, though, and in this ornery bolt bucket, maybe I should have figured five.

I pull off the highway at an exit for Round Rock and park under a gas station awning. I raise the hood and wave away a cloud of steam. The hose going to the radiator is leaking a little. I get the screwdriver out of the glove box and tighten the hose clamp taking care to avoid the hot radiator. Nothing to do now but wait for Old Gray to cool down and hope I make it in time.

I wipe a bead of sweat off my forehead with the sleeve of my shirt. Old Gray has the kind of air conditioning that only works when you're driving fast. My armpits are damp circles and the front of my shirt is spotted wet. So much for my first impression on the ladies. I'm hoping there will be a few good ones, though the camp information packet strictly forbids dating of any kind.

Thirty minutes later, I'm back on the road. The information packet I received in the mail says to be there at 2:00. I take exit 189 and pull into the T Bar M Parking lot at 1:58. The lot's full, so I find a place by a dirt road and park on the grass.

The building beside the parking lot is a basketball gym. A cardboard sign with an arrow above the word *coaches* is taped to the entrance. It points to a corridor that goes between the gym and another building.

I run down the path beneath a sign that says T Bar M and into another world.

The asphalt trail I'm on meanders through cedars and oaks to log cabin houses. On my right is a blue swimming pool and massive playground. On the left is the greenest grass field with a bright yellow football goal post and soccer goal at each end. A group of about fifty people are milling about in the middle. Across the field is a big two-story log building, the lower story open to the outside.

"Are you here for camp?" a girl sitting behind a table to my left asks. How did I miss her? I'm close enough to read the name "Suzanne" on her nametag.

"Yes." I extend a hand. "I'm Richie Wines."

Suzanne shakes my hand then looks down a list of names until she finds mine at the end and puts a checkmark beside it. She writes my name on a name tag. "We're starting in—" she looks at her watch, "—right now." She points to the field. "Everyone's already out there."

The crowd that I saw before is now sitting in a circle.

I put the name tag on and walk to the circle of strangers. They're athletic types around my age, with about the same number of men and women. They're talking amongst themselves as if they've known each other for years. I find an open place and sit. Am I the only one that doesn't know anybody?

A stout guy with an Arkansas shirt leans over and shakes my hand. "I'm Chevron."

"Richie."

"Where are you—"

The sound of screaming breaks up Chevron's question. We turn to look.

Two guys burst from inside the big log cabin building and sprint toward us.

The first guy's clothes, face, hair, arms, and legs are all the same bright primary red except for a large black *A* stamped on the front of his shirt. He must have used a gallon of paint to get that kind of coverage.

He makes the A sign above his head with his arms as he runs. "Alpha! Alpha! Alpha!" he shouts.

The second guy's an all blue Mr. T. clone minus the mohawk. His face and bald head are covered in blue paint and a blue cape billows in his wake. He runs with a fluidity of grace that seems out of place for someone his size. He makes the dog pound barking sound, puts his hands over his head in the *O* sign, and shouts "O-Omega! O-O-Omega!" between barks.

They run around the outside of the circle and are joined in their chants of Alpha and Omega by the college students around me. It's a convoluted pep rally where both team's fans show up at the same place and try to out-yell each other. The whole group is shouting either Alpha or Omega at each other at the top of their lungs.

What did I get myself into? I have to stand to avoid being the only one sitting. I notice that Chevron and a couple of others look as lost as me and feel a little better.

The Alpha and Omega guys are now in the center of the circle. They are each joined by a girl with the same kind of outrageous outfit. The girls' paint is a more sparingly used with an elegant red *A* on the Alpha girl's cheek and blue Greek Omega horseshoe sign on the Omega girl's cheek.

"Welcome to the Christ Centered Adventure," the Alpha man says. "This is going to be the best time of your life."

Suddenly Johnny appears and runs to the middle of the circle. "Wooooooohoooo!" he shouts. "Who's ready for some fired up and going nuts every minute?"

Everyone starts jumping up and down screaming hysterically.

Did I somehow sign up for one of those Pentecostal church camps by mistake? I didn't read the mission statement that close. Could I have missed something? Are they about to fall on the ground laughing or speaking in tongues?

"Buggala, buggala, buggala!" Johnny shouts.

"Ha, Ha, Ha!" everyone yells.

Dead silence.

Johnny lets the silence hang for a moment while he paces around the circle. When he passes by me he stops for a moment and winks. "This isn't one of those boring church camps you may be used to. Our motto is "Don't waste fun," and we don't waste a drop. We're gonna work hard, we're gonna play hard, and we're gonna live it all for Jesus Christ. Suuuweeeet! We're gonna make you into a bunch of Bible followin', kid lovin' machines. We got it going back and forth at the ropes course, the Sanctuary, the swimming pool, the basketball gym, the tennis courts, the baseball diamond, the rifle range, and everywhere else, all surrounded by God, all prayed for all year. There's gonna be miracles. There's gonna be changed lives."

Does Johnny need oxygen like the rest of us? He hardly stops talking long enough to breathe.

"Gotta go, but I'll be back in a while," Johnny jogs off the field and disappears behind the Gym.

"Spread your circle wider," the Alpha guy says. "Stretch your arms out and make sure you can't touch anyone. We're going to get to know each other."

The Alpha girl steps forward. "We're going to go around, say our name, say where we're from, what school we go to, and do a motion or action so others can remember us. Who wants to start?"

"I will." A girl steps forward. "I'm Kelli Conahan. I'm from Nacogdoches, and I go to Stephen F. Austin." She does a karate kick. "You can call me Kickin' Kelli."

"Action Jacks," someone shouts.

Kelli raises a hand with a two finger gun and smiles.

Good grief, what am I going to come up with for this thing? I'm used to a lot of tomfoolery—I go to A&M after all—but this place is a whole new level. I don't want to look like a complete idiot.

Jack does jumping jacks. Mike hikes a football. Liz crawls like a lizard. It slowly comes around the circle to me. I'm pleased to see that many of the girls are cute. The Aggies are greeted with a hearty whooping, so at least that will be something to look forward to. Everyone is so full of energy, so loud, and so confident.

None of them seem to be anything like me.

I'm still trying to think of something when it's on the guy next to me. He looks like a California surfer dude, or a Ken doll, with a big swoop of blond hair falling across his forehead. He jumps up and shouts. "I'm Jeff Dixon. I'm from Austin, and I go to *the* University of Texas. Hook em!" He sticks up Texas horn symbols with both hands, and takes off across the circle in a tumbling gymnastics pass, end over end, finishing with a flip and a full twist. "Yeah! I'm Gymnastics Jeff."

Everyone claps as Jeff returns to his spot.

I blink. How do you follow that? Rockin' Richie seems really weak now. They're looking at me. I have to do something.

I step forward, my legs trembling. "I'm Richie Wines. Fightin' Texas Aggie class of 1995." The whoops give me a little more courage. "I'm from Leroy, Texas."

"Leroy!" The big Omega guy, who introduced himself as Tailback TW, shouts. "Leroy!"

"Leroy," Gymnastics Jeff says.

I step forward, lie on the ground, do a weak roll to my right, and stand back up. "Rollin' Richie." It sounds more like a question than a statement. At the last minute I had thought that a parody of the gymnastics dude would at least get a couple of laughs, but could that have been any lamer? Now I look like a complete fool. I back up to my spot and sit down.

"Leroy!" TW shouts again.

The remaining members do their motions followed by another round of shouting Alpha and Omega before we break up into guy and girl groups. The guys head to somewhere called the Chuckwagon.

When we walk by the name tag table, Jeff grabs a name tag and writes *Leroy* on it in large block letters. He slaps it over my old name tag.

As far as nicknames go, I've been called worse. I follow the crowd into the Chuckwagon, which turns out to be a fancy name for the cafeteria.

If all this happens in the first hour, what will the rest of summer be like?

Richard Wines

Chapter Three

A New Strength

If I have to carry another picnic table, I'm going to collapse. I stop and put my hands on my knees.

"Come on, Leroy," Paul, my picnic table carrying partner, says. "We've still got half a trailer to go."

I groan. I've been at camp four days, and all we've done is work. Check that thought, we had a 10:00 PM worship session last night and a 6:00 AM Bible study this morning. They call the first week, "work week." Someone with an imagination came up with that one.

"Dude, who decided to make these things out of lead?" I ask.

Paul flexes a massive biceps and smiles. "Come on, it'll put some muscle on those bones."

I sigh. Easy for him to say, he's a college football player—a real athlete forty pounds heavier than me. I've worked construction and carried roofing shingles up a ladder all day, but even that's got nothing on work week. At least I earned five dollars an hour in construction. One of the guys calculated we made about fifty cents an hour here. Not bad if you're having fun, but this is work.

Paul and I follow the other guys assigned to picnic table duty to the trailer at the front of the property. For some reason they remove all the picnic tables at the end of each year just so we can bring them back before summer camp starts. There must be one hundred tables and only ten of us assigned to move them.

We heave another picnic table off the trailer and begin the long walk to the cabins. We'll drop this one off at Winchester, I decide. It's the first cabin on the trail and doesn't have a table in front of it yet.

Mike Goddard, the assistant camp director, walks up the path toward us. He's another ex-football player, a quarterback, and the most likely person on staff to play superman in a skit. I've never felt as wimpy as I do here. "Why don't y'all take that one to The Outback? We need ten more back there."

The Outback? My legs grow weak. This morning we moved several wagons of rocks around back there to make a new trail Johnny said we needed. The Outback's another 300 yards down the trail, past all the cabins, and across a little dry creek. It feels more like ten miles when carrying an 800 pound picnic table. Even Paul is breathing hard when I insist we stop and take a break. Paul's doesn't complain when I take a little extra time to catch my breath.

"Let's go coaches!" Johnny shouts from the Sanctuary. He's jogging again. He doesn't walk anywhere.

I'm not sure if he's talking to us, but Paul and I pick up the table and start waddling down the trail.

They call us coaches here because we *coach* sports to the kids that come. On the second day of work week, we're assigned a *specialty sport*, which is the sport we teach for the summer. Since they have a ton of tennis coaches, only girls do volleyball, and two varsity letters in football count for nothing against real division one college athletes, I got assigned the only logical thing a good ole boy from Leroy, Texas should do—Outdoor Sports.

For most specialties during work week, the three hours of specialty time are probably an easy walk through of practice techniques, reading through the playbook, playing a game of horse, or splashing in the pool. For Outdoor Sports, we have to mow and edge the rifle and archery range, move crossties, and repair the dilapidated awning over the area where we shoot rifles. Yesterday we rode bikes down all the camp trails, which might have been fun had I not been so tired. Today we got this *special* assignment to complete with the help of the football coaches.

Paul and I cross the bridge to The Outback and trudge the remaining fifty feet to put the picnic table under a tree beside two others.

I flex my hands open and closed. Muscles and tendons protest. How many more? There's got to be at least two tables left for each team on the trailer, but if we go slow, maybe only one. I take my time walking up the trail to the front of the property. Paul is already twenty feet in front of me.

Kylee jogs down the trail toward us. "They want everyone on the football field."

No telling what's going on. They stopped our work two days ago to have a full staff game of knockout in the gym. Anything's better than moving picnic tables.

We join the crowd of coaches milling about on the edge of the field.

Kelli comes out of the leadership cabin followed by Derrick, who carries an ice chest.

"Girls on this side." Kelli points as she walks toward us. "Guys on this side."

We break up into sides with the goal line between us.

"Spread out in a line and pick a partner on the other side."

We spread out in two long lines facing each other. I'm across from Liz.

What are we doing? Asking questions would be futile, the answers will probably confuse me further, so I put my hands on my knees and try to rest a little. I'm too tired to talk to Liz, even though she's one of the nicest girls in camp.

"We're doing a Farkle tournament," Kelli explains.

Farkle? I thought that was a dice game, but I don't see any dice.

"The team with the last one standing wins—" Kelli gestures to Derrick.

Derrick opens the ice chest and pulls out a two liter bottle of Coke. "Hooooooooch!" he shouts.

The crowd goes berserk jumping up and down like rabid animals.

I can't help but yell and go crazy with everyone else. I haven't had a soda since I got here. Candy and soda, *hooch*, are not allowed in Camp. Evidently that rule is broken on special occasions.

Derrick pulls out a Dr. Pepper. It looks ice cold and wonderful. I whoop like the good Aggie I am.

Farkle, as it turns out, is another word for rock-paper-scissors.

I face Liz. No smiling. This is for Dr. Pepper.

All along the line, people hold their hands out ready.

"On shoot," Kelli Says. "One, two, shoot."

I throw scissors.

Liz throws paper.

"Yes!" I shout. One step closer to Dr. Pepper heaven.

Liz grins sheepishly and backs away.

Those of us who won the first round square up against someone on the other team that won the first round as well. I get Jamie.

Jamie's all smiles. She's the bubbliest person I've ever known. "Scissors is a risky throw," she says, then laughs. Is her voice normally that high pitched?

I'm not going to let her psyche me out. "The rock rolls," I say. Let her think about that.

"One, two, shoot!" Kelli shouts.

I throw paper.

Jamie throws paper.

Dang, we're both out. If you tie in group competition both sides lose.

We're now down to five girls and four guys. The one extra girl gets to sit out while the other four go.

"One, two, shoot!" Kelli shouts.

Two guys win, one girl wins, and one tie. It's down to two on both sides.

Derrick pulls out the cooler and puts it between the contestants. "Don't get distracted now."

"One, two, shoot!" Kelli shouts.

Jason wins for the guys and Tatiana for the girls. The next round will be for Dr. Pepper.

Johnny comes running down the path from the front of camp. "Did I hear something about hooch?" He jogs to stand between the two contestants.

"Hooch to the winners," Derrick says.

Johnny frowns, appears to be in deep thought, and then his eyes light up. "What do the losers get?"

There's a moment of silence and then Jon Weems shouts, "Pool!"

A chant starts up, low at first. "The pool—the pool—throw 'em in the pool."

Johnny nods.

Kelli shakes her head no.

"The pool—the pool—throw 'em in the pool!" Half the coaches are shouting.

This place is so wacky it makes the crazy stuff that happens at A&M look as tame as Tuesday night bridge club at Aunt Ethel's. And this is with only so-called grown people here. What's it going to be like with kids?

"The pool—the pool—throw 'em in the pool!" The chant grows louder, and while many of the girls don't look too happy about the prospect, many are yelling just as rowdy as the guys.

Tatiana and Jason face off.

"One, two, shoot!" Kelli shouts. She's distracted, though, scanning the for an escape route.

Tatiana throws scissors.

Jason throws rock.

The guys' victory yell is deafening.

The girls scatter in all directions like a covey of quail when you flush it out from the underbrush.

Guys give chase and grab the slower girls before they get very far. They haul their kicking and screaming captives toward the pool, which is across the path from the football field.

I note a small group of girls that escape to the Sanctuary and follow. I guess I need to get at least one.

Kevin sprints past me and disappears behind several stacks of chairs in the corner of the Sanctuary. A girl screams. He comes out a moment later with Leah over his shoulder, hauling her like a sack of grain. She struggles in vain.

A door slams somewhere as I walk into the main meeting area. It's a wide open two-story space with huge log pillars to support the massive roof. This is where most of the meetings, like worship service and camp-wide teaching times, are held. Other than the support pillars, it's open to the football field and built so three-hundred people can run back and forth to the field in a short moment.

No girls to be seen. I'm ready for my Dr. Pepper, but this pool thing has now become more like hide and seek. I lean against a pillar to think. There are only three doors in here. One is behind the stage at the far end of the Sanctuary. The other two are the bathrooms.

I go to the girls' bathroom and pull on the door.

It moves a little, but feels like someone is holding it.

I pull as hard as I can.

The door suddenly flies open almost knocking me down.

Joy backs away from the door shaking her head. She's not one of the small wimpy girls like I had hoped would be in here, but a college volleyball player, strong and determined not to be thrown into the pool.

"This can be easy or hard," I say.

She locks her hands around a stall support and sits down on the floor. "Not going to happen."

Great, how am I going to get her out of here without hurting her or touching any of her inappropriate body parts?

To my relief, Kevin walks in. "Get her legs and I'll get her arms." He's done this before.

Avoiding a couple of nasty kicks to the face, I grab her feet and pull her outward.

Kevin pries her hands free and together we carry her out of the bathroom and onto the football field.

Joy fights the whole way, squirming and kicking, clawing and biting. Halfway across the field, I almost drop her. This is even harder than carrying picnic tables. Sweat pours down my face.

Most of the girls are already in the pool or climbing out. Kevin and I give Joy the heave-ho and with a yelp she splashes several feet beyond the edge.

I notice that the girls wearing white t-shirts are allowed to go back to the cabins to change into something darker before they go in. Propriety is the rule here.

The guys give each other high fives and laugh. Nobody looks to see if they can catch a glimpse of a girl compromised by the water, and nobody even talks about the possibility. And it's not because the girls aren't good looking.

I marvel that I don't even feel the urge to look and am suddenly ashamed that a week ago I would have broken my neck straining to see a little wet t-shirt action. This place is changing me.

Sweat drips off my chin. I look down at my filthy sweat-soaked shirt and jump into the pool myself.

By the time I climb out and get to the soda cooler, there's only half a cup of Dr. Pepper left. I savor every drop. Amazing how you take something so simple for granted.

"Picnic table crew, let's go," says Goddard.

I'm still dripping from the pool and my tennis shoes slosh beneath me. No time to go change, but at least I'll be cool. I follow the broad shouldered football coaches to pick up another table.

Five tables later darkness falls. I wolf down three sandwiches on the back porch and rush to my cabin to shower and put on dry clothes.

There's an all-coach meeting in the Sanctuary at 9:30. My steps are zombie-like and my vision blurs in a haze of fatigue. How could I be so tired? I'm the guy who used to sprint the half-mile back to the dressing room from the football practice field in full pads after doing red lines at the end of practice. I'm the guy who played eighteen games of sand volleyball from sunrise to sundown with no breaks to eat. I'm the guy who roofed ten hours in one hundred degrees and then played basketball until midnight. But my legs are wobbly, and when I get there I collapse to the Sanctuary mat. I don't know if I can take another step. It's 9:29.

The lights go down and the disco ball comes on. "Big House" by Audio Adrenaline plays at full throttle. All around me, my peers jump up and start clapping to the beat.

TW runs to his spot in the front and starts the motions of playing football in the back yard and eating food at the big, big table.

As one, the crowd joins in as if they're a bunch of crazed groupies at a rock concert.

Good grief. We've been working since 7:00 AM, can't we just have a quiet chorus of "Sanctuary" or "Holy, Holy, Holy?" I struggle to my feet, but I don't dance with the others.

For about the hundredth time I wonder what I'm doing here. I'm not like these people and don't have their energy. I've got a melancholy personality for crying out loud. I don't like public speaking, or making a fool of myself on purpose. And most of all, I hate being "Fired Up And Going Nuts Every Minute."

The song mercifully ends and I plop down on the mat. The lights go down for a skit. They even have a loud way of starting a skit here, where they pound on the floor and shout, "Sk-i-iittt, Lou-der," over and over.

Two guys walk on the stage. One is a nerd who looks like Urkel, and the other a cool guy named Spike.

I close my eyes and drift off as Spike plays a rude prank on Urkel.

"This is a special night!"

I jerk awake.

Johnny has replaced Spike and Urkel on the stage. He paces while he talks. "The leadership team and I have prayed for divine appointment. This is the moment you have been waiting for. Tonight—"

"Yes, Tonight!" everyone shouts in unison.

"—you are getting your first half co-coaches!"

The room erupts in shouts and whoops. We all stand up. "The Hey Song" starts up to more dancing, clapping, and the obligatory yelling of "Hey" after every other note. Does everything here always have to be so dramatic?

At the beginning of each of the two six-week summer sessions, co-coaches are assigned. These are people who share cabins, work as partners, and stay with the same group of kids. The first session goes from late May to early July, the second from early July to mid-August. Somehow I'm signed up for both—twelve weeks of adventure. Twelve weeks. I don't even know if I can make it through tonight.

Randy Sims, assistant camp director, joins Johnny on the stage. He reads off a piece of paper. "First up is cabin Buttercup. Jamie Dodson, come on down." He does a pretty good boxing announcer imitation.

Jamie screams, and runs to stand beside Randy. She hops up and down in excitement.

"Co-coaches Jenny and Leah!"

Jenny and Leah jump up screaming and run to meet Jamie who runs toward them. They embrace and spin in a circle yelling. When they pull away all three have tears in their eyes.

I couldn't be that excited if I had just won a new car.

Randy continues, "In Muleshoe we have the beef. Chaz, Beau, and Bill."

The three big guys stand, shake hands, and embrace. They shout a little, but at least they aren't crying.

Randy calls out more names to similar displays of excitement after each grouping.

I start looking at the guys who are left and consider who I'd like to be picked with.

"And next we have the Paaaaaainted Rooooock!" Randy extends the vowels. "Scott, Mitch, and Leeeeeeroy."

A spurt of adrenaline fills me and I jump up.

The three of us come together, give high fives and chest bumps. We embrace for a moment and sit down.

Mitch's eyes are rimmed with something surprising—weariness—the same weariness that fills me to the core.

I could have done a lot worse. Scott's a pretty boy with never a hair out of place, but he's a volleyball player and a nice guy. I'm in awe of Mitch. The three year starting quarterback for the division one North Texas Eagles, he looks and plays like Doug Flutie. I've seen him throw a football from goal line to goal line on the football field. I'm excited despite my tiredness.

When the remaining cabin assignments are complete, Johnny speaks. "These are the brothers and sisters you will sweat and bleed with for the next six weeks. Trust in each other, rely on each other, grow with Christ together."

The strobe lights begin and they start playing DC Talk's "Jesus Freak" at volume eleven. An impromptu mosh pit begins.

Scott jumps up and joins the moshing.

There's no way I can take any more of this. I groan and stand.

Mitch gets halfway to his feet and then collapses back to a sitting position.

I lean down beside him. "Are you okay?"

"Yeah, I just need a minute." He smiles weakly then his eyes roll back into his head.

I don't know what to do. I just stare at him.

Fortunately, Larry and some other coaches see what has happened and come to help. Together we pull Mitch out of the vicinity of the mosh pit to fresh air.

Mitch's eyes come back.

I sigh in relief. Maybe he just fainted.

"Breathe deeply," Larry says.

Cheri Polk, the camp nurse and Johnny's wife, rushes in and takes over. She starts asking questions and props Mitch up against one of the Sanctuary pillars.

Seeing that he's in more qualified hands, I walk to the back of the Sanctuary where the steps go up to the second level. The music is not as loud here. I sit and put my head in my hands. Mitch is a rock, a man among boys, and yet even he fell. In a way I'm glad, because I'm not the only one exhausted. But seeing Mitch collapse feeds the worries I've had all day. How am I going to handle this summer when a guy like Mitch struggles? My legs and arms feel like spaghetti, my lungs burn as if I'm breathing underwater, and my head aches as if it's the ball in a tennis match. My strength is gone.

I pray. *Lord help me. I don't think I have the strength to do this.* I can't say anything else. I'm too tired. I lower my head between my knees.

Like a gentle breeze, the formless voice stirs within me. *It is not your strength that you need.*

I sit motionless, not wanting the presence to leave, simultaneously terrified and full of joy. As the final chorus of "Jesus Freak" washes over me, a spring of new strength rises up inside. For the first time since I've been here, I don't feel so overwhelmed.

My fears of inadequacy, struggles to fit in, and dread of leading others are suddenly insignificant. I don't know what's going to happen, but this is where I'm supposed to be.

Maybe this summer will work out after all.

Chapter Four

Day Camp

Anthony throws another rock, narrowly missing the head of a kid on the monkey bars.

I run over, grab him by his shoulders, and hold him up to my face. "Stop throwing rocks at other campers."

He looks away, his eyes following someone in the distance.

I let him go and he's off onto the playground again. He stoops down and picks one of the small rocks that forms the base of the playground. He throws it at a tree in the distance and runs up the ladder toward the slide.

At least he didn't throw it at another kid. I sigh and give up. Why does anyone have kids when they're this bad?

It's Friday of the first week—day camp week. The kids don't live in the cabins this week, but instead they are dropped off every day by their parents at 8:00 and picked up at 4:30. The time between is a one hundred miles per hour blur of Fired Up And Going Nuts Every Minute (FUAGNEM), alpha, omega, chicken nuggets, sports, and a non-stop struggle to keep Anthony from killing himself or one of the other eleven kids assigned to Scott, Mitch, and me.

Anthony's been a pain from the beginning. He's seven, and I'm no doctor, but he's got to have ADHD or one of those hyperactivity conditions. He runs around with a wide-eyed crazy look on his face.

He's like a Doberman in a room with twenty cats. He doesn't know which one to go after, so he tears up the world trying to chase them all.

On Sunday night we drew names for small group and he was one of my four. I don't think he learned a single thing in the *Batter's Box* Bible study. It's a victory that his book has half its pages and my other three kids can remember what John 3:16 says.

Anthony slides down the slide and runs at me full throttle. Just before we collide, he pulls back a small fist and swings with all his might.

I've seen this trick before and catch his hand before he can connect below the belt. The first couple of times I had not been so quick. He laughs and runs to the monkey bars.

"Flood" by Jars of Clay blares over the loudspeakers signifying it's time for Team Meeting, the full camp gathering of singing, skits, and teaching. Since this is the last day, the parents will be there observing and have already been herded that way. The kids don't have to be told, they head to the Sanctuary in a dead sprint. All my kids are in front of me, all of them but one.

I spin around and find Anthony right behind me. "Come on, it's the last day."

Anthony looks up into my eyes. "I don't want to go. I want to stay here with you."

"But your mommy and daddy want to see you." And I'm going to kill you if you stay here.

Anthony frowns and puts his arms around my waist. "I don't have a daddy."

My heart drops, filling with guilt for my negative thoughts.

Anthony lets go and runs to catch up with the other kids. In Team Meeting I have to put him on my shoulders and let him sit in my lap to keep him from pushing the kids in front of us.

Later we meet with the parents and give a little presentation to each kid.

When it comes my turn to talk about Anthony, I describe him as "fun-loving, full of fire, and energetic."

His mom shakes my hand. "Thank you so much for a great week. He didn't give you any trouble, did he?"

I shake my head no. "Nah, he was fine."

She sighs, relief on her face. "Ever since the divorce he's been so—hyperactive. But this week has been big. He's gotten a lot better. He told me he wished he had a daddy like you."

I smile and don't know what to say. "Thanks," is all I can come up with.

Anthony hugs me and won't let go.

I hug back until his mom calls for him to go. As they walk away a little remorse touches me. Is it possible that I might miss him?

Richard Wines

Chapter Five

Dragon Blaster

Bill meets me on the path with a wheelbarrow and two shovels. "Let's go, Leroy. We've got woodchip duty." He tosses me a shovel.

I follow him down the path to The Outback.

Just because day camp ends at 5:00 doesn't mean we're done. Camp has to be cleaned for the next session. We get one day off a week, Saturday noon to Sunday noon, and they're going to get the most out of their fifty cents an hour before then.

Woodchips are as much a part of T Bar M as skits and peanut butter and jelly sandwiches. In The Outback, where they're clearing trees, a wood chipper and a ten-foot pile of chips wait for us. Cedars and live oaks cover much of T Bar M, and most of the large trees don't let enough light through for grass to grow. Every space on the grounds not covered by grass gets beautified by the chips, which is pretty much everywhere but the football and baseball fields. Woodchip duty is a never-ending job.

I'm heading up the main trail with my third wheelbarrow full of chips when Johnny runs up. "We're gonna go cheer for Randy at his softball game. The bus is up front." He points past the gym and runs down the trail to tell someone else.

Anything's better than hauling woodchips. I dump my load nearby and walk the wheelbarrow to the supply shed. My shirt's covered in woodchip dust and half soaked in sweat. I think about going back to my cabin to change, but see Johnny running to the front with a band of followers.

I jog to catch the group, about twenty-five coaches, and we load on the bus.

Some junkyard must have had a sale on 1962 model busses, because the bus is old and rusty, older even than the bus I used to ride to school back in kindergarten. It's already broken down twice in the two weeks we've been at camp.

Johnny whoops and throws the bus in gear. It jerks sideways, jerks back, sputters, then roars forward.

Fifteen minutes later Johnny pulls the bus into a baseball field complex. Four fields fan out from a circular drive and parking lot. Middle-aged balding men play softball on two fields visible from my window.

Johnny honks the horn, holding it down for several seconds before pulsing it in a one note off-key song that only he could know.

"Randy! Randy! Randy!" We shout from the bus and begin rocking it from side to side. All the windows are down and a couple of guys hang half their bodies outside. It's surprising how hard twenty people can rock a bus when you move from side to side in unison. Of course the bad shocks don't hurt our efforts.

Johnny pulls up beside one of the fields and jumps from his seat. "I'm going to find Randy." He runs to the field.

"Randy! Randy! Randy!" We continue chanting and rocking the bus.

The nearest softball game comes to a standstill. All heads turn our way. The umpire waves his hands in the air for the play to continue, but the entire infield has gathered around the pitcher's mound and point our way. None of them look like Randy.

"Hey, is that Randy batting?" Jason asks.

"It sure is," says Leah.

"Home run! Home run! Home run!" the whole bus screams.

I look at the batter. He's got the same stocky forty-year-old build as Randy, but with a batting helmet on there's no way to tell for sure. He turns to us and his face is different. Not Randy.

It doesn't keep everyone on the bus from shouting all the more. Once the typical T Bar M coach gets whipped into FUAGNEM frenzy, a small detail like a mistaken identity is not going to stop them.

Johnny jumps back on the bus. "He's not here." He scratches his head. "I'm sure he told me this was the place." He sits in the driver's seat, throws the bus into gear, and we're off again. Undoubtedly Randy told Johnny the wrong field on purpose, or he's hiding under the bleachers.

One of the girls starts a chorus of "Row, Row, Row Your Boat," and we rock the bus to the beat as we leave the parking lot. I don't see a person outside not looking at us.

We head back to camp through downtown New Braunfels.

At a sign that says *Comal River*, with an arrow to the left, Johnny suddenly makes a sharp turn off the road. A block later, he pulls into an empty parking lot and parks by a chain link fence. A glint of silver water flashes fifty yards beyond the fence.

Johnny kills the engine and turns to face us. He's got that mischievous look I recognize from my first interview. "Who's ready to run the Chute?"

A hearty affirmation goes up in the bus.

"Come on." Johnny opens the door and jumps outside. This should be interesting.

I follow with everyone else. It's about thirty minutes to sundown, and the sky is a deep blue painted with red, orange, and white streaks.

"Chute's closed," Jason says.

"No problem." Johnny heads straight for the fence. He climbs up the eight feet of wire near a *No Trespassing* sign and vaults over with the agility of an acrobat. "Come on." He motions with his arm for us to follow.

I look at Johnny. I look at the sign. Do I want to be arrested? Fifty feet down is an entrance gate. Maybe we can get in there. I run down but a heavy chain and padlock hold it closed. A sign to one side reads, *City of New Braunfels Tube Chute – Hours: 10-6.*

Most of the coaches are over the fence by the time I get back. Beau is on my side helping Joy get enough footing to go over.

Scott shakes the fence from the other side. "Come on, Leroy."

I climb the fence and jump over before I can talk myself out of it.

As soon as Beau is over, we follow Johnny across a green grass embankment down to the river. The sound of rushing water grows louder and the little dam that redirects the Comal River into the Chute comes into view.

The Chute is a glorified man-made water slide of concrete that redirects the Comal River down a twenty-foot drop through a couple of wide turns.

Johnny runs down the bank to the river upstream of the Chute and with a whoop, jumps in—shoes, clothes, and all.

The rest of us follow like lemmings.

An icy blast rocks my body.

My fellow coaches scream in protest. I never knew TW could sing soprano.

There's not much time to acclimate to the water temperature because the current of the river sucks me toward the narrow concrete alley that forms the Chute. I've done this before, but in a tube. Maybe this wasn't the best idea. There's nothing to help me float, and its hard swimming in my size thirteen shoes. My heart speeds up. Drowning is my least preferred way to die.

Johnny and the first of our group reach the Chute. They're swept down screaming and yelling.

My feet hit the bottom and begin to slide on the smooth, algae-covered concrete. The current strengthens as the first curve flows by.

The water depth shallows to waist deep and my speed increases. I wobble but remain standing around a big curve and see the rapids below where the Chute empties back into the river.

The last hundred feet are the steepest and the water shallows to mid-thigh. I fly across the moss bottom in my best surfer imitation and loose myself to the rush. "Yeeeee! Haaaaaaaa!" I give my best Dukes of Hazard yell.

The water shallows to knee depth and my balance becomes tenuous. I wave my arms madly, but it does no good. The final twenty feet are on my backside.

The end of the Chute hits me like an angry linebacker. The foaming water bounces me back, forth, and outward in a frenzy of overwhelming force. I try to swim but it gets me nowhere. I didn't take a good breath before going under and my lungs already burn. I concentrate on staying calm and let myself go limp. The water pushes and pushes and suddenly there's a lessening of current and my head breaks above water. Gasping, I swim toward the side where Johnny and several others wait on some steps.

Beau grabs my arm as I sweep past and pulls me up beside him.

My legs wobble and I have to sit for a moment to recover my strength. "Wow," is all I can say. That was fun, but I'm not sure I want to do it again.

As they come through the Chute, we help the remaining coaches up on the steps.

"Let's go." Johnny trots downstream after the last person is pulled from the water.

I follow, running to match his quick gate. He knows a way to slip past the fence down the river, which tells me he's done this before. We walk down an alleyway and a couple of minutes later we're back to the parking lot. The bus waits on the other end, a white speck a half-mile away.

The parking lot is on the edge of the Schliterbahn water park. Beyond the alleyway, a huge white water slide rises up above the trees and towers over us.

Johnny stops and looks up at the waterslide while we wait on the motley crew of wet coaches traipsing up the alleyway after us.

"We're going to ride that," Johnny says. "Wait here." He jogs toward a gate that looks like a service entrance below the waterslide. For a minute he knocks, then climbs halfway up the waterpark fence, raises his head over the top, and appears to be talking to someone. He jumps down, goes back to the gate, and disappears inside.

There's no way he's getting us on that thing. Schliterbahn's already closed for the day. I imagine the conversation he's having with some high school kid cleaning the park and laugh.

"What is he doing?" Eric asks. The rest of the coaches are milling about around me.

"Who knows?" I'm the only one who heard Johnny's plan, but telling them would only bring questions I can't answer.

Some of the coaches start walking back to the bus.

Johnny reappears from behind the gate, waves his arms, and yells, "Let's go!" A short, white-haired man stands beside him.

I run to where he waits at the gate. He couldn't have, but suddenly I'm not so sure.

"This is Hans," Johnny puts an arm around the man. "He's the engineer in charge of the *Dragon Blaster*." He gestures to the waterslide looming behind him. "This ride doesn't open to the public until next week, but Hans," he grins devilishly and pats the man on the shoulder, "has said that he needs some test riders. Any volunteers?"

I raise my hand and jump with everyone else, shouting my affirmation. Any tiredness I had from the Chute is washed away with the prospect of riding such an awesome slide.

Hans opens the gate and we file in.

Johnny winks at me when I pass. How could I have possibly underestimated him?

I grab an inner tube and head up the ladder to the top of the slide. The slide twists all over the place and I notice that in many spots it actually goes steeply uphill.

Sitting in a tube in a normal water slide feels a lot safer than surfing on my feet down a rushing river. Beyond the first turn is a steep drop. At the bottom of the drop waits one of the uphill sections. I'm wondering how my tube will make it up the hill when a blast of water slams into my back launching me uphill faster than I had gone down. My stomach drops at the unexpected acceleration.

"Wooo Hooo!" I yell as I'm launched over the top of the hill and start down again. In four more places water blasts from behind and sends me uphill. Past the final turn, the slide deposits me in a spray of water into an exit pool. What a rush.

The coaches who have gone before surround the exit pool. "Le-roy! Le-roy! Le-roy!" they shout.

I give a half-dozen high fives and a couple of chest bumps and join them.

One by one our peers splash down to louder and louder greetings as our numbers grow.

Johnny comes last to a roar of shouts and clapping. "God is good!" He shouts, waist deep in the pool. "Make sure you thank Hans." He climbs out to a barrage of back pats.

I shake Hans' hand on the way out the gate. "Thanks, that was awesome."

Johnny stands beside him explaining that we aren't just any camp, but that we're the "Christ Centered Adventure" because we follow Christ.

Ten minutes later everyone is on the bus and we're heading home again. The last remnants of purple daylight streak the western sky. A chorus of "Lord I lift Your Name on High" starts up.

I lean back and close my eyes. I've always dreamed of the Christian fellowship and acceptance I've read about in the Bible but never experienced until now. I feel so unworthy to be included in the company of these people with their kind eyes and servant hearts. But the grace that surpasses all understanding is real. By that grace I'm somehow here, not as an acquaintance, but as a partner, friend, and co-coach. I'm overwhelmed by the sweetness of the moment and soak it in, thanking God and praying for it to last.

"Farm-co, Farm-co, Farm-co!" A chant begins.

I open my eyes. We're on highway 46 almost back to T Bar M. In the distance the lights of the Farmco gas station come into view. My throat's suddenly parched. The memory of an ice cold Dr. Pepper makes me lick my lips. I join the chant.

"Farm-co, Farm-co, Farm-co!" We scream.

Johnny looks in the mirror back at us. He's going fast, but at the last possible instant he slams on the brakes and swerves into Farmco.

A cheer goes up.

Johnny parks the bus and everyone files out.

I stay in my seat, still awash in reverie. I'm afraid that if I move, the bus will turn back to a pumpkin and all this will be gone.

Johnny walks back and sits beside me. "What are you waiting for, Leroy?"

"Just thinking."

"That was pretty cool, wasn't it?"

It was the coolest thing I'd ever done. "Yeah."

He puts his arm around me. "You know you're one of my favorites."

I look into his eyes. They dance with the mischief and joy I've come to recognize in my short time knowing him, but there's something else there. Sincerity. This hyperactive, crazy, sold out, godly man is becoming one of the most influential people in my life.

He slaps me on the back. "Let's go get a soda."

I follow him off the bus.

By the time I get a Dr. Pepper at the fountain machine, Johnny and the cashier are cackling with laughter. "That makes me think about how much Jesus loves you," he says as I walk out the door. "Do you know Him?"

The Dr. Pepper may be the best I've ever had. Every drop is like heaven on my lips.

Johnny comes out of Farmco and we're on the road again.

One of the girls starts "Awesome God" by Rich Mullins.

I join the song this time, not worried I'm a little out of tune. The words ring true. Halfway through the chorus I realize this might be the best day of my life.

Richard Wines

Chapter Six

Skirtball Wars

"The targets are that way!" I shout. "The gun stays on the ground!"

Jackson points his rifle back toward the targets at the end of the range.

In Outdoor Sports the kids shoot from the prone, or lying flat, position. From prone position, the gun can't easily be pointed to the side. This precaution doesn't keep some of them, like Jackson, from trying. These are .22 caliber rifles, and while they may not take down an elephant, they're still deadly.

In high school I played tennis. I won my district championship as a senior, and at twenty-one, am still a decent player. I thought I'd be a valuable asset to a camp with the tennis credentials of T Bar M. Wrong. They took one look at my resume, saw Leroy, TX, and put me straight into Outdoor Sports.

Outdoor Sports is three things: riflery, archery, and mountain biking. They were correct to assume that someone from Leroy would be proficient at these disciplines, but I enjoy tennis more. When I asked to be a tennis coach, they told me they had plenty of tennis coaches, but that Outdoor Sports needed help. I agreed—with the caveat that I'd have the option of changing mid-summer.

Outdoor Sports is the only specialty held away from the main camp. Twice a day, we load up an old 1982 Ford Econoline van with the twelve kids on riflery and archery rotation to take the mile and a half trip to the "Outdoor Sports" area. The rifle range and archery range are set up on one corner of a fifty-acre piece of land filled with cedars and mesquites.

Ben and the six kids that went to the archery range walk up. "Ready to go, Leroy?" Ben's a big guy a little off center from the rest of the coaches in camp. He had a stroke when he was a teenager and one side of his body doesn't work quite right, but he laughs a lot and has the kindest heart I know.

"Last shot," I say.

The kids shoot and retrieve their targets while I pack the guns.

Ben and his group wait in the van. He and I are both new coaches assigned to Outdoor Sports with Dan Yarbrough as the specialty head. Dan trains us, works with us for a couple of weeks, and suddenly leaves camp. In his absence we are assigned Dan Grider as a helper. Grider hasn't been rifle certified like Ben and me, so we put him in charge of bikes. Four weeks into summer, Outdoor Sports is coached by two rookies and a substitute stuck with eighteen maniacal 7-13 year olds who don't know the difference between a .22 and a water gun.

After my kids and I load into the van, Ben turns the key. It sputters, jumps and dies. "Whoa Betsy," he says. The name had stuck when he used it during our first week. "Why don't you drive? Betsy likes you better."

I shrug and swap places with him.

On our twice a day trip to and from the Outdoor Sports area, we pass several tennis courts where campers and coaches play tennis. When we drive by today, Tennis is drinking water, or more likely Gatorade, from Dixie cups. Classical music plays from a jukebox. They've got new water jugs, fresh towels, and good-looking female co-coaches. It wouldn't surprise me if they had fruit, bagels, and orange juice out there. And they don't have to worry about getting killed in their specialty.

I realize that with the coach shortage in Outdoor Sports, there's no way anyone's letting me change specialties mid-summer. "Dang tennis players," I say.

"Yeah," Ben says. "Dang girly skirtballers. We could take 'em."

I laugh. I've never heard that term before.

Ben rolls down his window. "Skirtballers!" His voice has a loud grating quality.

Tommy and Elizabeth look up from their drinks.

Ben climbs out the window and sits on the windowsill. "Skirtballers in skirts!"

The kids in the van perk up and look out the window. I can't decide if I want to join him or duck down and hide.

Tommy picks up a tennis ball and hits it toward us.

The ball sails over Betsy, missing Ben's head by a couple of feet.

"Skirtball!" Ben shakes his fist and slides back into the van. The kids and I are laughing, but Ben's dead serious. "We're going to get those skirtballers."

So the battle begins.

The next day the kids are talking about skirtball before we even get into the van. On the way to the range, I roll down all the windows.

The tennis players are already starting their drills. A crowd of them, at least thirty, and six coaches are on the courts. They don't notice as we drive the van into an adjacent parking lot.

The kids start rocking Betsy back and forth with Ben's guidance. "Wim-ble-don Wan-na-bes! Wim-ble-don Wan-na-bes! Wim-ble-don Wan-na-bes!" They shout out the window facing the courts.

Ben climbs on the window ledge so that he's standing with his hands on the roof. "Go back to England you bunch of skirts!"

Amber, Elizabeth, and Susan along with most of the tennis players who didn't see us yesterday drop their jaws in shock.

I peel out, putting a six-inch strip of rubber down on the parking lot as the chant of "Wim-ble-don Wan-na-bes" continues from the kids in the van. I wonder if we're going a little too far, but the kids are having so much fun and Ben—well I haven't seen this much life out of him since we met.

At Ben's request I leave the range a little early to make sure Tennis is still in session when we drive back by. Ben has spent most of the session making something out of long leaves of grass at the edge of the rifle range. He has it in his lap in the passenger seat. I don't ask because I'm not sure I want to know. The windows are all down when the tennis courts come into view.

"Skirt—ball!" Clap-clap-clap. "Skirt—ball!" Clap-clap-clap. The kids yell repeatedly. They're really into it. I wish I could cover my ears, but I need to hold the steering wheel.

Tommy and Seth look up from their practice, malice in their eyes.

"Stop!" Ben says.

I slam on the brakes. Ben jumps out of Betsy, puts the grass around his waist like a hula skirt, and starts doing a hula dance on the side of the road.

Three kids join him in his mock luau to the frenzied chants of "skirt-ball" from the van.

I'm laughing so hard I miss the fact that Tommy and Sean have taken a ball caddy and ten kids through a side gate of the tennis court.

"Fire!" someone yells.

I look up to see ten yellow tennis-ball missiles heading our way.

"Duck!" I shout too late.

One of the balls nails Ben below the belt. Thwack! Thwack! A couple others slam into Betsy.

"Retreat!" says one of the hula dancing kids. They run to the van.

I open the door for Ben. "Get in!"

Bent at the waist and limping, Ben plops into the passenger seat. "Fire!"

Thwack! Thwack! Thwack!

The final kid, Jackson, gets into the van holding his leg. At least he's not crying.

I slam Betsy into gear and speed away as another volley of tennis balls slams into her broadside.

Ben holds a fist out of the window. "You won't get away with this you skirts!"

I park Betsy and check on Jackson. He's already showing off the welt on his thigh like a badge of honor. What if that had hit him in the head?

"We've got to get 'em," Ben says. "Look at what they did. We got to take it to the next level."

The kids shout their agreement.

"This thing is getting out of hand," I say. Way out of hand. "We're going to let it cool down."

Everyone groans, but I stay firm.

That afternoon, I drive the long way to and from the range and avoid the tennis courts altogether. Maybe it will blow over. Even Tommy seems overly friendly that night at dinner. I'm relieved he's not taking any of this seriously.

The next day, Ben and I are on the way to Betsy with our kids when Grider runs up. He's a stout, red-headed guy, probably the only other coach as crazy as Ben. "The bikes are gone."

I stop. "What do you mean the bikes are gone? They were in the storage room last night."

"There not in there."

"Johnny must have let someone borrow them."

Grider holds out a piece of paper. "I found this."

In the center of the paper is a crudely drawn figure of a rifle, a bow, and a bike with the words *Outdoor Sports* under them. A circle with a thick dark diagonal line is drawn on top of the whole thing. I blink. Seriously?

Ben grabs the paper. "It's the skirts. They got our bikes."

Shouts of protest go up from the kids.

Ben rips the paper up and then wads it into a ball. "This isn't right. We're going after them."

I hold my hand up in the air. "We'll get 'em, but let's fan out and find the bikes first."

We assign groups of three to look over every section of camp. The bikes can't be that hard to find, there's twelve of them after all.

I'm searching The Outback when Jacob, one of the older kids, runs up. "We found them way back behind the screamer. They're all tied up."

I round up my search crew and we head that way. Tied up? That doesn't make any sense.

At the screamer, a giant ropes course swing, I see Ben and the others back in the woods. The bikes are all around a big tree with a rope going through their frames tying them to the tree and each other. When I look closer, knots are tied every few feet in the rope and they're on top of a big Prickly Pear cactus. What a mess.

Ben, Grider, and I huddle away from the kids.

"We can't let them get away with this," Ben says.

"No stinkin' way," says Grider.

This has already gone too far, but Ben is right, we can't let them get away with this. I've been a tennis player, so I try to think like them. Yelling and mocking them might put them off their game, but it has no lasting impact. What is something that would screw up their practice? Suddenly it comes to me.

"I've got an idea." I look at the bikes, to Ben and to Grider. "Ben, go to the Sanctuary supply room and get some of the costumes, like the skirts and dresses. Grider, take several kids and go to the maintenance shed and get as many wheelbarrows as you can. Meet me on the Back Porch in ten minutes."

"What are we doing?" Ben asks.

"I'll tell you on the Back Porch."

Ben and Grider take off to their tasks.

I set to untying all the knots and getting the bikes free. I keep eleven kids, one for each bike. This idea may land us in trouble, but sometimes you do what you have to do.

My hands are full of cactus thorns, but with the help of the kids, I'm done in fifteen minutes. We each choose a bike and ride to the Back Porch.

Grider and Ben are already there. They've found four wheelbarrows and a pile of clothes. We circle around a picnic table and I go over the plan I've dubbed *Operation Outdoor Sports Strikes Back*. Ben will lead the skirts, I'll lead the cavalry on the bikes, and Grider, with the three biggest kids, will lead the garbage men.

The cavalry heads to The Outback with the garbage men. We fill the four wheelbarrows to the brim with T Bar M special wood chips. I toss a couple of shovels of dirt and gravel in each for good measure. We take the back road from The Outback. If anyone in leadership sees us they will certainly ask, and I don't want to explain.

We gather at Betsy for final instructions.

Ben is dressed in an afro, bell-bottoms, tank top showing his flabby midriff, and a hula skirt. He's got a real tennis skirt from somewhere and ties it to Betsy's antenna. His three kid helpers are dressed in similar outfits. I really hope Johnny doesn't show up now.

"The operation is a go," I say.

"Yeah!" Shouts Ben. He gives everyone high fives, loads into the van with his kids, and is off.

I turn to Grider. "Give us some time to distract them before making your move."

The tennis courts are only about a quarter mile away from the parking lot. The eleven kids on bikes follow me and we take a shortcut across the baseball field to get there.

Ben's already at the courts. He's out of the van doing his little dance, yelling, "my skirt hurts," in his grating voice.

All the Tennis kids and coaches are looking his way when we ride onto the tennis court. I find the first ball caddy and kick it, sending balls flying everywhere.

"Hey!" yells Robert. Robert, Vu, and Tommy start chasing us around the courts as we topple more ball caddies.

The kids yell, "skirt-ball, skirt-ball, skirt-ball!" We let Vu think he's actually chasing us away.

At that moment, Grider and his three helpers sprint onto the other side of the court with their wheelbarrows full of dirt and chips. They run to the center of the court, dump their loads of woodchips, and run away.

"Mission complete!" I yell and pickup my speed. Tennis balls fly as we ride away at full speed. Fortunately, we're out of range before the skirtballers can put up much resistance.

The whole Outdoor Sports crew meets at the Back Porch. We've pulled it off, with the only fall-out being a skinned up knee and a flat tire on a wheelbarrow.

"Those skirts should know better than to mess with us," Ben says.

True, they got what they had coming for stealing our bikes and tying them up, but I'm not so sure about it now. Perhaps the dirt on the courts was a little over the line. If Johnny, or heaven forbid, one of the Turpins finds out, we'll be in some serious hot water. Tennis is the pet sport here. They get treated with a higher preference. I've no doubt which side the directors will take. But the look on Vu and Tommy's face when they saw the dirt—priceless.

That night at dinner, Tommy bumps into me while I'm on my way back from the kitchen with a plate of food. I almost drop it. I wonder if he has something planned in retaliation. But what could he do? The bikes are doubly locked this time. He might go out to the range and trash the place, but how is he going to get out there? And when is he going to find the time? No, he's just mad because we one-upped him. Nonetheless, the lump in my stomach gets bigger.

Half the kids in my cabin are talking about what we did. When they ask me about skirtball, I just shrug and say nothing.

The next morning we gather for specialty time and head out to Betsy. I grab the rifles and walk with Ben and the twelve kids behind the Chuck Wagon to the parking lot.

Jackson and Mason stop in front of me gaping. Jackson points to Betsy.

What are they doing? "Come on, get in," I say.

The sun moves out from behind some clouds and shines on Betsy like a beacon pointing to a lost treasure, like a golden scepter of blessing, like—

Betsy has no wheels.

I stop and blink. What the heck?

In place of Betsy's wheels are cinder blocks and short pieces of two by four. All four wheels are gone. Disc brakes and wheel bolts are the only things left.

Ben walks up to Betsy, rips his shirt off and throws it on the ground. "Those dang skirtballers!" He's so angry he sprays spit. "This is war!"

The kids join his uproar. "We're gonna go break their rackets," Jackson says. He mimics Ben by taking his shirt off and throwing it.

I keep staring at Betsy's wheels. We must have really gotten to them. I realize it's probably the best prank that's ever been played on me. No doubt Tommy and Sean did it. They are the only ones over there with enough gumption and mechanical skills to pull it off. I imagine Tommy under Betsy at 4:00 AM with the wimpy little jack from his Honda Accord trying to get the thing to go high enough to take the rim off the full size Econoline van. The thought of the strain on his face makes me double over with laughter. He's lucky he didn't kill himself.

"It's not funny, Leroy," Ben says. "We've got to retaliate."

Yes we do, but how are we going to top this? We aren't. I can't tell Ben and the kids, though, they have to believe we are getting the best of skirtball. "We're going to get all the water guns out of the Sanctuary, all the water balloons out of the leadership cabins, and the water-balloon launchers from under Mark's bunk. Prepare for *Operation Skirt Splat!*"

"Yeah!" the kids shout.

"And get all the cans of shaving cream you can find," Grider adds. I don't want to know what he is planning. This could get ugly.

An hour later, I crouch behind the condo beside the tennis courts.

Eighteen kids, ages eight to fourteen, huddle around Grider, Ben, and me with nervous anticipation. Most are clothed in Camo with faces painted black. Each has been assigned one of two groups, artillery or infantry. The infantry each have a Supersoaker 1000 water gun or higher. Jackson has a model 20000, complete with dual spray hoses and a five-gallon holding tank that he wears on his back. The artillery stand beside two wheelbarrows full of water-balloons and a bucket filled with "special" balloons.

Ben is dressed the same as the kids, but wears a hula skirt over his blocky behind. His face twitches in a snarl. "Let's go."

Dan is dressed in all black, his face, arms, and red hair painted black.

We've got to get this done now. Our scout, Jimmy the baseball coach, told us the entire skirtball specialty is on these two courts. "Take yours around to the west side," I say. "Wait for us to loosen them up and then you can cross between condos without being seen. I draw a diagram in the dirt. "Charge in and then we'll have them surrounded."

Ben nods and heads off with the infantry.

I set the timer on my stopwatch.

The kids in artillery prepare the two water-balloon launchers standing apart like I told them. I stand behind one with a wheelbarrow of about fifty balloons in front of me and Grider stands behind the other.

At sixty seconds on my watch, I nod to Dan. We load the first balloon and let fly.

My balloon hits the roof of the condo, and Dan's goes way off to the right.

"Calibrate," I say.

The second balloons lob straight over the condo.

"Shhhh," Grider says.

Someone screams behind the condo.

I nod and we send wave after wave of balloons over the condo, as fast as we can let them go.

After ninety more seconds I figure Ben has to have made his move. "Phase two. Go."

I grab three water balloons and run between the condos toward the tennis courts. Two kids bring the wheelbarrows of balloons from behind

The scene at the courts is mass chaos. Outdoor Sports kids are chasing Tennis kids and spraying them with water guns. Tennis kids are tossing cups of water at Outdoor Sports kids and filling them up at their water coolers. Ben runs after Kate spraying the back of her head.

I throw my balloons at the closest targets. The first one misses, the second hits Grant in the back of the head and bounces off, and the third hits Tommy's tennis racket, drenching his left side. I run back to the wheelbarrows and get some more balloons.

The other artillery members lob balloons into the melee, though they probably hit as many friends as foes.

Grider sneaks around the side of the court. He smashes one of his special balloons on Vu's head, covering him with the contents of our secret weapon—shaving cream. He gets Kate and Robert and then a wrestling match ensues, spilling the contents of his bucket onto the court. He falls and disappears under a melee of arms and legs.

A Tennis kid grabs a shaving cream balloon and hits an Outdoor Sports kid in the back.

Mason runs across the growing shaving cream puddle and wipes out.

Sean emerges from one of the condos, a water hose with a spray nozzle in his hand. He turns it on and starts blasting everyone who comes near.

I concentrate my fire on Sean. One of the balloons hits, but bounces off. He turns to me and sprays. I'm drenched before I can get away. Even Jackson's gun can't stand up to that.

When I turn around, Vu, and some Tennis kids have discovered the wheelbarrows. One is already tipped over and the other guarded by two kids fighting a losing battle against five. The second wheelbarrow falls to the ground and most of the twenty or so balloons inside burst on the grass. I grab two that survived and head back to the court.

Kids on both sides scoop shaving cream up from Dan's bucket spill and sling it at each other. Ben runs over to get a handful. While he's bent over, Tommy and Robert rush at him with a water cooler.

"Watch out Ben!" I yell too late.

They dump the cooler of water on his head.

Ben slips and falls on the slimy mess under his feet.

Grider roars and stands up, throwing Tennis coaches and kids off him. Shaving cream and black paint run down his face, arms, and legs.

Things are way out of hand here. There's going to be a real fight if this goes on too much longer.

"Outdoor Sports, fall back!" I shout.

Most of our kids run my way.

Ben struggles to his feet, slips and falls, then crawls toward me. "Fall back!"

Grider stumbles off the court. He looks like the Staypuff Marshmallow Man after taking a wallow in a mud pit.

At the fallen wheelbarrows, I count troops. "We're missing one kid."

Grider and Ben look over the group.

"Jackson," says Grider.

I look back to the courts.

Jackson is circling the court spraying people with his giant water gun.

Unlike skirtballers, it's no man left behind in Outdoor Sports.

"Jackson!" I run out to get him. I pick him up and sprint off the court under a barrage of tennis balls. Shaving cream splats on my arm. Sean hits us with his water hose, drenching me further.

I stumble but keep going and soon we're out of range. I put Jackson down and we jog to meet the rest of our group halfway across the baseball field. With all the congratulations and high fives, you'd think we won the battle. I guess it depends on your point of view.

The next morning I'm sitting at a Back Porch picnic table with Ben, Grider, Tommy, and Sean. Johnny paces in front of us.

"I got a call yesterday from a family staying in the condos by the tennis court. They said there was a riot going on." He pauses. "A riot?" He puts a hand on his forehead and shakes his head. "One of those kids could have been hurt and what am I going to tell the parents, 'Little Suzy broke her leg in a riot?' or 'Little Timmy got his eye put out by a water balloon launcher?'"

Can't say I didn't see this coming. I try to calm my heart. I've always been a wimp when it comes to discipline.

"Anyone want to explain?"

I keep quiet. I don't really know what I'd say anyway. What did happen? It all seems so stupid now.

No one says anything.

"A kid came up to me this morning and asked, 'What is skirtball?'" Johnny continues. "Next I'm going to have parents asking me." He sighs. "And what if the Turpins hear? I might expect some of the other coaches, but you?" He keeps his eyes on me for a quiet eternity.

I lower my eyes. There goes my favored coach status. Johnny's never been so serious. I wish I could crawl under the table. I shift my weight. The bench seems extraordinarily hard.

"I didn't believe it when Goddard told me about the van. Of all the crazy stunts. And what if it fell on you or someone else? I had to pay the maintenance guy fifty bucks to put those wheels back on." He puts a hand to his mouth. Did he just smile? He looks away for a moment and then back to us, an obvious fake frown on his face. "Your Covenant leaders will work out your punishment." He puts his hand back over his mouth, coughs, and abruptly walks away.

That Saturday during specialty time with the parents, half the kids mention skirtball. Ben and I laugh nervously and don't talk about it. Jackson says that it was the most awesome week of his whole life.

After the kids are gone, the five of us get a work project hauling woodchips on our one day off. A pretty light punishment all things considered.

One of the camp administrators approaches me as I'm heading out for dinner that evening. "What did you guys do in Outdoor Sports? We had fifty kids sign up for it next summer."

I laugh. "Just had fun I guess."

She smiles, starts to walk away, and then hesitates. "What, exactly, is skirtball?

Chapter Seven

True Purpose

"Now kids, it's time to settle down and start huddle time," Vincent says.

The kids immediately stop what they're doing and move to form a little circle in front of Vincent. They keep their hands in their laps, mouths shut, and eyes focused. They're eight years old.

I've seen this all week but still marvel. None of my kids from the first half of summer ever acted like this. I'd be lucky if they weren't scalping me by now. But this is the second half, and Vincent's my co-coach.

Jeff, my other co-coach, sits across from me. The astonished look in his blue eyes tells me he's thinking the same thing.

"What did you learn tonight?" Vincent asks. He's got a soft, even voice and I'd have thought him a mousy, thin wisp of a guy if I'd heard him over the phone.

At least half the kids raise their hands, but none speak.

Vincent points to Dylan. Vincent's forearm ripples with a hundred muscles I never knew existed in the human body. His loose shirt can't hide the bulges underneath. He's got muscles on muscles and not one ounce of body fat.

"Jesus," Dylan says.

"Good," says Vincent. "What else?" He points to James.

James lowers his hand as if he's surprised to be picked. "About God," he says shyly.

Vincent smiles as if that were the best answer in the world. He's a twenty-seven-year-old college graduate and teacher of special needs kids during the normal school year. He's got patience, discipline, godliness, and runs a 4.5 second forty-yard dash.

"Jeff, what did we learn?"

Jeff sits up. Vincent often asks Jeff or me questions in huddle time as a way of keeping us involved. "We learned that we need Jesus in our hearts."

"Good, Jeff. Can anyone tell me why?"

Ryan raises his hand, the only hand that goes up.

Vincent points to him.

"We need forgiveness from sin."

Vincent smiles and claps his hands. "Yes, exactly right. We have all sinned." He grabs a flashlight and puts it on the floor in front of him. He walks his first two fingers in the light like a little man. "We were made to walk with God in His light. But we all sinned." He puts the fist of his other hand in front of the light and walks the finger man around behind it in the dark. "The sin keeps us from God." The finger man runs into his fist, but can't get through. "But God so loved the world that He gave His only Son. Can anyone tell me who God's Son is?" He scans the raised hands. "Dylan, do you remember your answer from earlier?"

Dylan smiles. "Jesus."

"Yes, and whoever believes in Him will have life. Our sins are forgiven by Jesus." He raises his fist away from the light. "All we need to do is ask for forgiveness and believe in Jesus." He walks his hand in the light. "And we will know Him."

The room is quiet but I feel the unseen power of the Spirit of God all around us. I'm conscious of every breath.

"Richie, when did you believe in Jesus?"

Lord, help me to say this right. I take a deep breath and am taken back to when I first believed. I remember how the Spirit of God poured into me at that moment like a million rivers. Almost the same as what I feel now. "I was a kid, about the same age as you guys. I told my mom and dad that I wanted to accept Jesus into my heart. We knelt on the floor and I prayed for Jesus to forgive me of my sins, and I asked Him into my heart." Tears pool in the corners of my eyes. I get through it without breaking up—barely.

Vincent smiles. "The Bible says that you need to say with your mouth and believe in your heart that Jesus is Lord." He stands up. "Richie, Jeff, and I are going to go into the coaches' room right over here. If you've never accepted Jesus into your heart and you want to accept Jesus into your heart, come into our little room and tell us." He turns and walks to the small coaches' room in the middle of the cabin.

Jeff and I follow. The three of us clasp hands and Vincent says a quick prayer. "Lord if it be Your will, please save Your little children tonight." The power of God is so thick I'm surprised I can even breathe. The skin prickles on my neck and arms.

Dylan walks through the door. His face is lit with an angelic smile, his eyes full of joy. "I want to accept Jesus."

James follows behind Dylan. He comes over to me and hugs my leg.

"Do you want to accept Jesus?" I ask.

Big brown eyes look up at me. "Yes."

Bryan and Will follow.

"I want to pray," says Bryan.

"Me too," says Will.

Vincent laughs and claps his hands. A tear runs down his face.

All seven of us kneel on the floor in the little room.

Vincent leads each boy in a prayer. "Jesus, I believe that You died on the cross and rose again. I know I have sinned. Please forgive me of my sins, and come into my heart."

After each has prayed, we stand up and hug.

My legs are weak, but at the same time there's a raging fire of power surging through me. I sit down in a chair and bow my head, absorbing the moment, reliving what it was like know Christ for the first time all those years ago.

"Are you okay, Leroy?" Vincent's hand is on my back.

I stand and wipe away tears. "Never been better." As I follow him into the main cabin I realize this might be the best day of my life.

Chapter Eight

Rainy Day

"Alright boys, we've got to come up with a name for our team," Glenn says.

It's Wednesday, the middle of week, the tenth camper session of my second summer. Things start to get a little repetitive the tenth time through for full-summer coaches. The same chubby bunny competitions, the same songs in worship time, the same churros and refried beans at Sunday night dinner, and the same Wednesday camp-wide Olympics competition.

"The Cowboys," says Greg.

"The Redskins," says Billy.

"The Longhorns!" says Cantor.

"No!" Glenn and I respond at the same time.

Glenn and Seth are my co-coaches for this half, and Glenn is a fellow Aggie. We've got eleven and twelve-year-old kids this time. They're a great age, independent enough that we don't have to help them get dressed and not quite old enough to have a teenage attitude.

Why is it so hard to come up with a name for our relay team every week? We always settle on something like *The Terminators* or *The Commandos*. Glenn can take it this round. He seems to care more about it than I do.

On Wednesdays we don't have specialty time. On the surface that would seem to be a good break from boredom and a chance to take it easy and catch up on rest—but this is T Bar M. On Wednesdays it's FUAGNEM all day with no naptime or FOB (Flat on Bunk).

I hate Wednesdays.

The kids are arguing over whether to call our team *The Transformers* or *The Pirates*.

"Leroy, what name do you like?" Glenn asks.

Both names are lame. "Neither. Pirates are a bunch of scurvy beggars and Transformers are so 1986."

"Scurvy beggars?" Cantor asks.

"What's scurvy?" asks Seth.

Glenn tilts his head sideways. "It has a ring to it."

"It was a joke." I say.

"Who votes for *Scurvy Beggars*?" Glenn asks.

All twelve kids raise their hands.

It's the lamest name we've ever had. I think I like it.

The relay begins with a team cheer. All the cabins form a wide circle around the three judges, TJ, Susan, and Otto, who sit in chairs in the middle of the field. We get fifteen minutes to develop our cheer.

We huddle together and Glenn lays out a plan. When Kelli blows the horn, some cabins are still practicing, but we've got our cheer down cold. It doesn't exactly take a lot of training. We run back to our spot on the circle.

A cloud covers the sun and a breeze blows in from the north cooling my sweat-soaked skin. Maybe it won't be 100 today after all. Gray clouds billow above the trees in the northern sky.

Kelli, a battery-powered megaphone in her hands, stands in the middle of the circle with the judges. "The first event is the team cheer. Each team has one minute to perform for the judges. First place gets 100 points, second 50, and third 25." She turns in a slow circle. "Remember that at the end of the day whoever wins the most points gets a hooch party!"

Kids jump up and down screaming. Four days without candy or coke is a long time for a kid. Heck, it's a long time for me. I wouldn't mind winning that party.

"First up is Sweeeeetwater!"

A pocket of girls on the other side of the circle scream and run to the center. They're one of the younger cabins, maybe eight or nine years old.

"Sweetwater, Sweetwater, Mmmm, Mmmm, Mmmm." They rub their bellies. "Sweetwater, Sweetwater, good, good, good." They mimic eating something. "Sweetwater, Sweetwater, sweeter than you." They pose. "Sweetwater!" they shout and all start screaming and doing cheerleader kicks.

"Great job, girls," Kelli says. "Next cabin is Muleshoe."

Seth walks up to me and Glenn. "We're five away." He holds up a bag of marshmallows. "I'll pass these out when we're two away."

"Don't give them more than two," I say. They have to be able to yell.

Seth nods and hands me and Glenn two marshmallows.

Painted Rock does something where the kids curl up into balls and roll around, which isn't too bad, but otherwise all the cheers are lame. Many of them do the same thing their cabin did last week. Their coaches are obviously losing creativity in week ten.

When we're two cabins away from our turn, I put the marshmallows in my cheek and see all the kids doing the same. I give Billy a thumbs up. "Don't eat it."

"Gun Barrel," Kelli says.

"Alright boys," Glenn says, "forward march."

The kids follow Glenn and me in two rows, stepping to the beat that Seth claps out. When we reach the judges' table, the kids line up in ranks behind us.

Glenn and I lead Aggie yell leader style, and the cheer begins.

"S-C-U-R-V-Y! B-E-G-G-A-R!" We hold the R for a long second just like the Aggie yell. "Beggars Left, Beggars Right, Scurvy Beggars We're all Right!" We pause. "Ready, aim, fire!"

"Drool!" I yell and let part of the half-dissolved marshmallow out of my mouth.

"Beggars drool, beggars drool, beggars drool," the kids chant and walk around like zombies randomly moving to all parts of the circle. Marshmallow drool flows down each face.

Girls scream and back away.

Boys laugh and point.

"Okay," Kelli starts on the megaphone before our drooling can go on too long. "that—was Gun Barrel."

I spit out the rest of my marshmallow. Hope that cheer doesn't get me another work project.

A girl screams to my left.

Cantor is still in his zombie state, arms raised, foot dragging, stalking Buffalo Gap.

I run over and grab him. "Good job, but we're done."

The kids give each other high fives and shake hands.

"We're going to win." Billy says.

"Yeah," Greg says and everyone else agrees. But I don't know. TJ and Susan had sour looks on their faces.

Ten minutes later, all the cheers are done. The judges and Kelli huddle at the judges' table.

Kelli breaks from the table and yells into her megaphone. "The judges have made their decisions." She waits until there is silence. "In third place—is Muleshoe."

The Muleshoe boys do their dog pound barks. TW's one of their coaches, and it seems that every week his kids take on this way of cheering.

"In second—is Painted Rock."

Painted Rock chants "Rock, Rock, Rock."

"We've got to win," says Greg.

My heart pounds. Do I really care if we win? It's just a dumb cheering contest. In ten weeks I've never won, but suddenly I have the feeling that we just might have a chance.

"In first place—is Sweetwater!"

The Sweetwater girls scream, jump and holler as if each had just won a million dollars. They run in circles hugging each other. Really? You've got to be kidding me. They weren't even in my top ten.

"We were robbed," Glenn says.

Seth throws his hat to the ground. "The contest was rigged."

The kids moan and gripe along with my co-coaches.

I feel numb. But why should I be surprised? I knew they wouldn't appreciate what we did. Even when we try something different it's the same predictable results. No wonder I don't like Wednesdays. Now if John Weems and Chris Ray had been the judges, things might have worked out.

A raindrop hits my head. I look up to see dull gray clouds above and darker skies to the north. Two more raindrops hit me in the face. Across the field, rain taps on the gym roof like a thousand tiny snare drums.

Girls scream and run from the field, some heading to the Sanctuary, some to the gym.

I'm already soaking with sweat, so what does a little rain matter? The soft drops refresh my parched skin. There's no lightning or thunder. Let it come. Maybe we won't have the Olympics today.

Seth and a couple of kids run back to the cabin, but Glenn and the rest are still on the field. Most either stare up at the sky or walk around in circles. The rain is not the window-rattling deluge of a thunderstorm like what normally hits here in summer, but the lazy patter of a shower good for watering grass.

Billy runs to the side of the field and kicks a soccer ball toward me.

I stop it with my foot and dribble toward the soccer goal at the back of the end zone.

The Winchester cabin mills about nearby. Kids laugh and many have arms outstretched and mouths open catching raindrops.

I kick the ball to the goal.

Jase, Winchester coach and soccer player, intercepts my weak kick and heads the other direction.

"Hey," I say. "Give that back!"

Jase looks over his shoulder. "If you want it, come get it."

I run after him. That little premature-balding, short dude is not going to show me up. The rain patters on my face and my shirt is already soaked through. I'm gaining on him.

At about the fifty yard line, Jase cuts to the right.

I don't go with him, but instead cut the angle toward the goal. When he turns again, I'm right beside him. I give him a hip check and he stumbles away, but somehow manages to maintain his balance and keep the ball. I'm sure that was a foul, but what do I know about soccer?

At about the twenty yardline, Jase taps the ball with his foot and stops.

I plant a foot in the wet grass, but it slips out from under me as if I stepped on a banana peel. I wipe out, arms flapping to no avail.

Jase takes two steps past me and leisurely kicks the ball into the goal.

I'm not a soccer player. How am I supposed to compete with him? Nonetheless, my competitive blood burns and I want another shot. I had been dead tired before, but now it's as if the rain drops are energy and I'm overflowing. "How about a game, your cabin verses mine?"

"Sounds good," Jase says. He grabs the ball and runs to the fifty yard line motioning for his cabin to meet him.

I call my guys and Glenn over. The game is on.

The rain continues its steady rhythm.

No one bothers playing soccer positions. We all follow the ball like a bunch of four-year-old first time players.

Glen breaks away and scores for our team, Jase for theirs.

As we play, new people join. Soon, our ten-on-ten is twenty-on-twenty, then forty-on-forty. No one is officially given sides; instead newcomers just play for the team that needs the most help. Someone turns on the Sanctuary speakers, and Stephen Curtis Chapman's "The Great Adventure" booms out into the rain.

I take my shoes off. Things get a lot more slippery, but I'm more agile without the rain-sodden, size-thirteen shackles on my feet. I feel like Icarus flying over the field. After an hour my legs are still as fresh as when we had first begun.

Eric steals the ball from another kid and kicks it my way.

I streak down the field, water splashing beneath my feet.

Hoomook comes out of nowhere and bumps me in the side.

I give him an elbow and he falls away. It's just me, and the six kids playing goalie. I kick the ball above their outstretched hands. Goal!

A ragged cheer goes up, but scoring is so frequent, it doesn't warrant a lot of celebration. I don't even know what the score is.

Jase runs into the goal, grabs the ball, and starts it the other way.

Glenn comes over and gives me a high five. "Awesome, man!"

The field is a soggy mob of kids and coaches—there must be at least one hundred fifty people. I can't believe that none of the directors or leadership has come out here and stopped us yet. They must know that the camp Olympics aren't going to happen and realize this is a good alternative.

I'm reminded that one of the camp mottos is *Don't Waste Fun* and am ashamed of the negative attitude I've had the last few days. But even that, the most ingrained part of my former self, is being transformed and washed clean by the gift of a rainy day.

I follow Glenn back into the fray. What a place this is.

Chapter Nine

Jam Session

"Su-per-Mike! Su-per-Mike! Su-per-Mike!" the whole camp screams at Team Meeting.

I laugh when I notice that the coaches are shouting louder than the kids. The rain has stopped and everyone from my cabin is dried off from the awesome time of soccer on the field. I'm awash in the mellow endorphins that come after hours of heavy exercise doing something you love.

The lights go down and Supermike, Mike Goddard, begins another adventure on the projector video. He's coaxed into a heavily modified circus cannon by the absent minded professor, Ollie. Supermike's all smiles and thumbs up until the cannon launches him toward a kids swimming pool. He overshoots the pool by a mile, and to his horror, finds himself among the targets at the Outdoor Sports archery range. "Dueling Banjos" starts playing.

Ben, dressed in overalls and holding a bow, yells, "Fire!"

Supermike runs for his life while arrows fly at him from all angles. The camera jumps to the point of view of an arrow as it closes in on Supermike's backside. Supermike screams.

The scene breaks and we see Supermike with an arrow sticking from his rear limping down the road back to camp. The Supermike music starts as the picture fades and the lights go back up.

That video always makes me laugh. Something about Mike's face and Ben's psycho yell. The twelfth time and it's still as funny as the first.

Johnny runs up to the stage. He's got his hand behind his back. Strange, he's never done that before.

"The Tongue," Johnny says. "Is the source of all kinds of evil." He pulls his hand from behind his back.

He's holding a cow tongue. It's about a foot long and six inches around at the base. It looks like a miniature Jabba the Hut.

Kids and coaches scream. Some turn away while others stare in fascination. I'd guess that ninety percent haven't seen a cow tongue before.

Johnny walks to the left of the stage. He holds the cow tongue up to his face and pretends like it's his tongue. "First you tell a little lie here." He waggles the end of the tongue. "Lie, lie, lie." He walks to the other end of the stage. "Then you talk about a friend behind their back here." He waggles the tongue. "Gossip, gossip, gossip." He walks to the center of the stage. "Pretty soon, you're not obeying God at all. Slander, slander, slander." He walks out into the crowd.

Kids and coaches scramble to give him room.

"If you don't control your tongue, eventually you're saying bad things about God." He waggles the tongue. "Blasphemy, blasphemy, blasphemy." He leans down and walks to one side.

Girls scream. The crowd clears a wide radius around him. He has that glint in his eye, and nobody wants anything to do with that cow tongue.

"You've got to cut off that tongue," Johnny says. He pulls out a pocket knife and acts as if he's cutting the cow tongue from his face. He holds it outstretched away from his body. "You've got to get rid that evil tongue." He throws the tongue across the room. It lands up front between the stage and the Sanctuary matt.

A cabin of girls in the front row shriek and run away.

Brittney, one of the girls' coaches, crawls backward as if the tongue is a rattlesnake poised to strike.

Johnny strides over and picks it up. "All sorts of animals have been tamed, but the tongue—" He holds it out in front of him and acts as if it is attacking him. "—has never been tamed. Don't let it rule you." He struggles with it, stumbles, and falls down. He grapples with it on the floor then rises up and tosses it out of the Sanctuary into the bushes.

Team meeting ends and the kids are quickly in bed and sleeping after lights out. They're so tired they don't even complain. We've had a good bunch this week.

Seth is already in bed when I go to the coaches' cabin.

I'm not ready for the day to end, but one of us has to stay in the cabin with the kids and Glenn isn't here. "I'm going out. You good?"

He grunts.

I take it as assent and head outside. Kids' curfew is at 10:00, coaches at 10:45. I look at my watch. 45 minutes.

On the porch of Winchester, Crag Miller tunes his banjo.

"Going to play?" I ask.

Craig picks a few notes. "I got a little somethin' brewing. Sit down and stay a while, Leroy."

I sit down and listen. The banjo is an exotic instrument, the twangs and fast moving notes mesmerizing. The rain has stopped and the air is cool for the first I can remember all summer. Crickets play backup to the banjo.

Mike Spratt arrives with a guitar case and sits beside Craig. He pulls out a guitar and strums a chord.

"I'm a-pickin'," Craig says.

"And I'm a-grinnin'," Mike says. He plays another chord and Craig joins in.

I recognize the song. "Sweet Home Alabama."

Craig starts in on the chorus right off the bat. It's the same notes and rhythm as "Sweet Home Alabama," but the words are different.

"I'm agin' dancin'.
You had better be as well.
I'm agin' dancin'.
It'll send you straight to hell."

I laugh but that was a little confusing. What does the agin' mean?

As if reading my thoughts, Craig stops. "An old lady in my church came up to me one day and asked, 'You guys ain't doin' no dancin' in that youth group a yours, are ya?' I tell her no and she says, 'Good, cause I'm agin' dancin'. That dancin'll send you straight to hell.'" He smiles and starts back in on the chorus. "I wrote this song in her honor."

It makes a lot more sense when I realize that the *agin'* is a backwards Arkansas way to say *against*. We aren't even that hick in Leroy.

Mike joins in on the guitar.
"I'm agin' dancin'.
You had better be as well.
I'm agin' dancin'.
It'll send you straight to hell."
Tim and two other camp All Stars walk up and sit on the porch. They're a group of high school kids that do a lot of the hard work around camp for nothing but room and board and the privilege of being here.

Chris, music leader and rock star wannabe, arrives.

Craig turns and points to Chris. "Dancin'—you for it or agin' it?"

Chris laughs and scratches his chin. "I figure I be agin' it." He speaks in the slow drawl of Grandpa Ray, one of his skit personalities. He must have seen this bit before. "That dancin'll send ya to hell."

"Preach it," Craig says and starts playing again. "Here's how it works gals and fellas, you come up with the verse and we all sing the chorus."

"I've got one," Chris says.

"Alright then," Says Craig. He and Mike sing through the chorus and start the song over.

Chris begins.
"You can lie or cheat or steal,
Or even misbehave,
But if you start that dancin',
You'll end up ten feet in the grave."
We laugh and all sing the chorus.
"I'm agin' dancin'.
You had better be as well.
I'm agin' dancin'.
It'll send you straight to hell.
By this time a small crowd has gathered. Grider and Ben, Tommy and Glenn, Liz and Rachael.

"Whose got the next one? Craig asks.

"I got it," says Glenn.

He sings his version, then Liz, then Tommy. They're all good. Everyone sings the chorus with our voices louder after each verse. Someone starts singing harmony and the notes blend in that mysterious magic that makes a song more than the sum of its parts. Craig picks the banjo in a complex contrast to the simple guitar chords. All his notes are in perfect time and tune.

I try to think of a verse myself, but can't quite come up anything of the quality that the others are putting out.

"I got one," Says Ben. He shakes his head to the rhythm of the beat. This should be interesting.

"Even if you're dancin',
In your room all alone,
You had better stop that dancin',
Or they'll be hellfire and brimstone!"

He shouts the last line screamo style like a thrash rocker.

I laugh so hard my stomach aches and I almost fall out of my chair.

Craig stumbles in his picking and loses the tune. He tries to speak, but laughs instead and the song dies without the chorus.

Grider gives Ben a high five. "Yeah! You rock!"

The crowd around the porch, now about twenty-five people, is laughing uncontrollably. How is it that we're not waking up the whole camp?

Craig recovers. "That, my friend, was incredible." He looks down at his watch. "We have time for one more."

Grider steps up on the porch. "I got it."

Crag and Mike start the song and Grider begins.

"You may think that dancin's okay,
But I tell you you're a liar.
Cause if you keep on dancin',
You'll dance right into the lake of fire!"

He screams the last verse.

My side aches and I get the hiccups I laugh so hard. How could something so stupid be so funny? I don't understand, but it's the way of this place. I join the last chorus.

"I'm agin' dancin'.
You had better be as well.
I'm agin' dancin'.
It'll send you straight to hell."

Craig keeps playing and we go through the chorus again.

I close my eyes and let the river of song take me. I don't want this day to end. These friends are different. They don't care that I'm a goofy kid with a heavy Leroy, Texas accent or that I'm awkward and sometimes say what I think. They're my brothers and sisters.

This day I want to hold inside somehow, to save these feelings for a time when things are less than perfect, when I can bring them out to remind me of the inexpressible sweetness of life. The hard work, the tedious routine, the hours of dealing with unruly kids—they're all worth this moment. This might be the best day of my life.

Chapter Ten

Leaving

I walk down the long path out of camp with my backpack on my shoulder. The rest of my things are already in Old Gray for the trip home.

"Not Enough," by the little known Texas group Caedmon's Call, blasts from the Sanctuary speakers. How many great songs and groups has this place introduced me to? The Caedmon's Call CD that Ollie gave me might be my most valuable possession. The songs remind me of the times, the people, and the faith that have characterized my experience.

Damon walks by heading the other way. He puts out a hand. "Stay in touch, Leroy."

I shake it. "I will."

He hurries off to whatever errand he is on. The final session starts in two hours and preparations are underway.

The weight of finality hangs heavy on my shoulders. Part of me wants to go. I've got a real job starting in Washington D.C., and my plane leaves in two days. But will I ever be more alive than I am here? My heart tells me no.

I feel like the kids in the Chronicles of Narnia when they grow up. I've become too old for this fantasy land and now I have to go. Sure, I'll return, but it will be different. I'll be a visitor, not a resident. When I walk out that gate, a chapter in my life is gone—perhaps the greatest chapter.

Each step brings another memory, each step harder than the one before.

There's Alex, the fourteen-year-old kid who had considered suicide until he came to camp and learned to live for Christ.

There's The Hillbilly Holler, a place I seemed to fit in well.

There's the trip to Lake Travis where all the hamburgers were eaten, so I had two plates of beans. The next day was less than pleasing.

There's the shock on six-foot-ten Will's face when I beat him in a one-on-one game.

There's the time that fourteen other coaches and I dressed up in camp costumes and drove into town in a single car, went bowling, and went to the grocery store.

There's riding in boats at the Riverwalk

There's Chaka, the friendly ape boy from Land of the Lost that grew into a camp legend after I told Outdoor Sports that he lived in the woods, and then the all-camp meeting a week later with Randy telling us that kids were having nightmares because they believed a man eating ape named Chaka was stalking them.

There's Whitney, the first girl in Outdoor Sports, who taught me what LYLAS means.

There's my whole Batter's Box praying to receive Christ.

There's the camp WWF wrestling spectacular.

Some of the memories are silly and some are serious, but all are T Bar M. They pile up until I'm overwhelmed. I stop on the path and try to compose myself.

Johnny drives his old diesel truck down the service road on the other side of the football field. He rolls down the window. "Leroy! Come here!"

I walk across the field. Maybe I'll get to tell him goodbye after all.

"Get in," he says.

The smell of the truck, the old leather, dust, and kerosene always reminds me of my grandfather's truck. It also reminds me of all the talks I've had with Johnny on the trips to town, to his house, or a quarter mile down the camp service road. For some reason he likes to take me with him.

These times are the most precious to me, when I see the real person under the personality. In the truck he's mellow, almost laid back. In the truck, I'm not an employee, or a person to charm with his antics, but a friend in Christ.

Johnny looks ahead and sighs. "So you've got a job?"

"Yeah. Amazing that they let me delay my start by almost three months. I've never heard of that before."

Johnny looks at me, the spark of knowing in his eyes. "Everything is amazing that He does." He points to the sky.

I nod. The amazing is commonplace when it comes to T Bar M. "I'm going to miss this place."

"You know you've always got a home here."

I fight back tears. "It's been a good run, a really good run."

Johnny reaches over and hugs me. "You've always been one of my favorites."

A tear gets by my defenses and rolls down my cheek. "You don't know how much that means."

More memories pour over me.

The time I met him under the old oak in the woods and he explained Psalm 39.

The time I tried to tackle him behind the Chuckwagon so we could throw him into the pool. I needed ten other coaches to help me.

The wacky way he'd get the the whole camp to sing "Happy Birthday" to the same maintenance guy every week.

The time he ran out on a tennis court with the giant T Bar M prop racket and tried to play tennis with two ladies.

The way he treats everyone the same no matter the job or station.

The way he always makes me feel as if I'm strong, smart, and important.

Of all the things about T Bar M, I realize he's going to be the hardest to live without.

We sit for a long minute of silence looking over the football field and I take it all in one last time. I give Johnny a second hug and leave the truck before I'm bawling.

"You're gonna make us proud, Baby!" he shouts as I trot away.

To my relief Old Gray sputters and starts when I turn the key. I pull out of the parking lot onto highway 46 and start the three hour, or maybe five hour, drive to Leroy.

Richard Wines

Afterward

Fifteen years later I'm on the field again. It's the last night of Family Camp.

Emily, my eight-year-old daughter, kneels before a rough-hewn cedar cross that's been placed on the field after Team Meeting. She's crying.

The skit at the end of Team Meeting moved her deeply. I'm not sure if she's sad or happy and guess that her tears are simply a response to the unexplainable, awesome power of God that moves here. I feel the power myself, like the fierce wind at the onset of a thunderstorm, and my tears join hers.

My wife, Jennifer, and I put our arms around Emily. "It's okay." I say. "He did this because He loves us. It's important to have these feelings. Then we can appreciate what really happened." I pat her on the back.

"Because of this we can have joy," Jennifer adds. "Remember that He is risen."

Emily nods.

"How about some milk and cookies?" I ask. "They have some on the Back Porch." Family Camp still has its perks.

Emily wipes her eyes with the back of her arm and stands on wobbly feet. "Sounds good."

I stand with her and give her a big bear hug. The three of us walk hand in hand toward the Back Porch.

Not much has changed in fifteen years other than a couple of new water slides, a new cabin, and more tennis courts on one side of the field. Walking down the winding asphalt path is like walking through a time warp. We pass Winchester, where Craig and Mike played their song, and past the tree planted in Mike's memory.

Johnny's voice rises above the crowd of people milling around drinking milk and eating cookies. I can't quite understand what he's saying, but could I ever really understand him? He bounces from group to group, like a bee in a garden of flowers, never staying in one place for long.

I look to the field and almost see Jase behind a soccer ball, sprinting across the spot where I did my "Rollin' Richie" ten minutes after arriving that first day. On the far side of the field, the tree planted in his memory sways in a breeze.

The breeze hits us, cool and refreshing after a sweltering day. The hairs on the back of my neck stand up. How is there always a cool breeze here at night? It feels almost supernatural. No doubt if druids had discovered this place they would have built a ring of stones.

But we have something greater than mysticism, something as solid as the beams of cedar that form the cross. When our time comes we'll be more than trees of remembrance. Our journey will just be beginning. That is what this place is. A preview. A prelude. A window into what will be.

Encore

Disclaimer:

I've come to believe that God has a sense of humor as infinite as His other attributes. This divine wit leads to an array of circumstances that can only be described as infinitely incomprehensible.

Of all the things that happened to me at T Bar M, one story gets the most requests for retelling at reunions and gatherings with old alumni. I initially left it out of *T Bar M Coach* because it didn't flow with the other stories, didn't have any spiritual purpose, and is quite frankly, far from *the best day of my life*.

Those who dare read on should be warned that there is no edification, redemption, warm and fuzzy feelings, or musings of nostalgia here. The only reason I included this story is because I don't want to field years of questions about why it *isn't* here. I'm hopeful that after more than fifteen years, the statute of limitations has run out. Read at your own risk.

Richard Wines

The Ride

We make choices every day. What clothes will I wear? What will I eat? Will I be friendly? Should I buy this house? Can I hold it to the next rest stop? Should I write this story? And so on.

A choice can change the entire course of a day—or a life. Ironically, sometimes the smallest choices—the choices we give the least amount of thought—make the biggest impact.

Grider, Ben, and I stand outside Betsy with 14 kids ready to go to the Outdoor Sports rifle range for afternoon specialty time.

"Hey Leroy," Grider says. "Mind if I drive Betsy today?" He holds his hand out palm up.

I start to reach into my pocket for the keys but hesitate. It's the second half of my third year and Grider's never driven before. Why? A warning bell clangs in the back of my head. I try to think but draw a blank. It feels as if I'm missing something important. He has a license. He drove here, and he has a car. What's the big deal? Besides, if Ben can drive Betsy, anyone should be qualified.

I look at Grider and scratch my head. He's a stout brick of muscles with fiery red hair and constellations of freckles typical for someone of his complexion. I've always been a little intimidated by him. As a teenager, he was the leader of a big city gang. Converted in high school, he is fully committed to Christ. But some of the street swagger remains, and he's probably the toughest guy at camp. His background and occasional edgy unpredictability are the only objections I can come up with. That would seem a shallow premise for denying his request, especially when the trip is so short and boring.

And so I make my choice.

"Alright." I hand him the keys. "Treat her right."

We pack tight into the Betsy. We're skipping bikes for a round of *fruit and vegetable shootout*, a favorite of the kids, so all of them are here.

Ben sits in the passenger seat and I move behind him in the first of Betsy's three rows of bench seats. I make Mark, a scrawny kid about twelve, move over so I can sit by the doors.

Grider cranks Betsy with her usual spurts of protest. He revs her loudly. When he looks in the mirror to back out of the parking space, I see an eager gleam in his eyes. The warning bell clangs again.

At the tennis courts, we make the obligatory stop to taunt. We're forbidden to get out of Betsy now, and Tennis is forbidden to hit balls at us, but we are going to annoy them the best that we can.

"My skirt hurts! My skirt hurts! My skirt hurts!" We yell while Grider turns Betsy left and right in an imaginary slalom. He hits a speed bump sending me flying out of my seat. My head hits the roof.

"Yeah!" Ben shouts.

"Ouch!" I say.

The kids cheer. At least I made them all wear seat belts. I rub the sore spot on my head and hastily buckle up.

Ben sits up on the windowsill. He pulls a pink tennis skirt out of the glove box and waves it around in circles above his head. "My skirt— it hurts so much!"

Grider jerks the van to the left.

Ben flails his arms and starts to fly out the window, but he catches the mirror with his right hand. His feet and legs stick straight in from the window. There's more of him outside than inside.

I reach out to grab him and Grider swerves Betsy the other way.

Ben shoots back through the window and plops into his seat. He's laughing in that funny silent laugh he has, and I catch myself laughing too. But it shouldn't be funny. He could've been hurt.

"Betsy Rocks!" Grider jerks Betsy back the other way. When he gets to the edge of the road, he doesn't turn back but veers off into the grass—straight for a basketball-sized rock.

Betsy's front left tire scales up the rock and does a wild bounce as it comes down. A loud thump emanates from her underside as Grider pulls her back onto the road. That couldn't have been good. We're only going about ten miles per hour, but I wonder if the tire might go flat. On most cars it would. But Betsy recovers and drives on as if nothing happened.

"Yeah!" Grider shouts.

The kids cheer and Ben gives Grider a high five. "Betsy's a beast!" Ben says.

"She's a tank!" says Grider.

Between the tennis courts and the range is an upper-class residential neighborhood. As we drive through, Grider lays on the horn. Lawn crews look up from their mowers, old men stare at us from porches, and joggers crane their necks to see what's causing the ruckus.

Thankfully, someone had the foresight to put speed bumps about every two hundred feet. These provide just enough deterrent to keep Grider from testing Betsy's top speed. As it is, my seatbelt saves my head several more times.

I put my hands to my ears. Betsy's horn and the screaming kids are testing the limits of my eardrums. This is getting out of hand.

About halfway through the neighborhood, Grider swerves into the circular driveway of a large home. He speeds up instead of slowing down.

An older lady watering flowers in the yard looks up, shocked disbelief on her face as we barrel through her driveway and under an awning by the house's front entry.

Ben gives the Texas Tech guns up salute and shouts something indistinguishable over the horn. Great, the lady probably thinks he gave her the finger.

I give silent thanks when we reach the turnoff to the range. Grider has to stop on the little gravel road while Ben unlocks the gate that admits us to the property. I let myself relax a little. We should be safe now. Just another hundred yards and we'll be there. I'm working on a way to get the keys from Grider before the trip home.

Grider starts the van down the road a few feet then stops. We don't normally close the gate while were down here, so what's he doing? He points off to the side of the road at a mountain bike trail. "Betsy's a tank. Who's ready for some off road?"

What does he mean by *off road?* You can't take a vehicle down there. It's about a four-foot-wide bike track over jagged rocks through a forest of cedar trees.

"No!" I shout. But I'm drowned out by fourteen hyperactive kids who have no idea what they are asking for.

"Cool," says Ben. But I hear a hint of apprehension in his voice.

Grider looks back and I catch that wild glint in his eyes. I shake my head back and forth.

71

"Betsy's indestructible!" Grider shouts and veers the van onto the bike trail.

The high-pitched wail of tree branches on metal shoots chills down my spine. Many of the branches snap as we pass through. What's a hundred more dents and scrapes to go with the tennis ball dents already in Betsy's side? We turn a corner. A tiny grove of four-inch saplings stand in a small island in the middle of the trail. There's no way we can make it any further. Surely he sees that.

"I think she can make it." Grider turns straight into the trees and jams on the accelerator. Betsy's front bumper hits the trees and they bend forward like tall blades of grass. They scrape, shriek, and thump on Betsy's undercarriage, but she rolls on.

The trail turns rocky and goes down a small steep valley. Betsy bucks over boulders and uneven rocks that would be difficult to traverse on a mountain bike. I wish I had a mouthpiece to keep my teeth from snapping together. How can her tires be holding up?

Ben puts his arm up like a cowboy and yells over the screams and laughter of the kids.

We reach the bottom of the valley and Grider guns Betsy uphill. The trees narrow out and suddenly we're driving through the open expanse of high grass behind the rifle range. He slows down and steers toward the place where we normally park.

I sigh in guarded relief. Do I dare hope this journey is over?

Grider lets out a wild laugh, swerves Betsy to the left and speeds up.

A huge prickly pear cactus rises above the grass, directly in our path. It explodes into a million pieces on Betsy's bumper and grill. Green cactus pieces splatter the windshield. The roof vibrates as pieces land on top of us.

"That rocked!" Mark shouts.

It was pretty cool, but what must Betsy look like? How are we going to make her presentable again after this little trip?

Grider bangs his head to some inaudible heavy metal track and continues to speed forward beside the rifle range. He turns on the windshield wipers and scrapes away a remnant of cactus in an aqua smear.

Something nags at the back of my mind. Something I should remember about this patch of grass. Then it hits me. Ben and I moved several old crossties here during work week. All this grass had been mowed then—two months ago. "Stop!" I shout.

Too late. Betsy's front end jerks up violently and bounces us skyward. A moment later the back wheels do the same.

Grider hits the non-anti-lock brakes and the wheels slide. We run over a second crosstie, a third, and a fourth. It feels as if we're in a popcorn popper at the moment all the kernels pop at once.

Betsy finally comes to a stop right in our regular parking spot but facing the other way. I look behind me and ask if everyone is okay. The kids are laughing and high fiving.

"Rad ride, dude," Mark says.

I unbuckle and move toward the door. "Let's go." There's no way Betsy's suspension should have survived that.

"Betsy's invincible!" Grider says. He puts Betsy back in gear and pulls forward.

I'm thrown back into my seat. "Whoa!" There's got to be something I can do to get out of here. And I don't think we should drive Betsy anymore without at least checking her out. "Aren't we going to shoot up the fruit we brought out here?"

"Yeah!" A kid behind me yells.

Grider slams on the breaks and stops. "Who wants to take Betsy for a ride around the pond?"

A cheer goes up all around me.

Not good. Fruit shoot out isn't going to compete with that. I've got to pull out the trump card, the last trick I have up my sleeve. "Who's ready for Capture the Flag?" Kids always want to play Capture the Flag.

A half-hearted assent goes up, not nearly as lout as the cheer Grider got. Dang, I can't help it if he's a better salesman. I know he's not going to go for a leisurely drive, not after what has happened already. But I don't know how to make him stop. It's not like I'm his boss or anything.

Grider pulls Betsy forward. He drives her past the driving range and archery range down a dirt road about a half mile to where the road splits at a large clearing in the trees and circles an old stock pond that must have once been used to water cattle or for fishing. The pond's fishing days are in the past, however, because at this late day in the summer it's nothing but a stagnant pool of black water ten feet across and maybe a foot deep. A ring of sun-cracked black dirt surrounds the water with waist-high grasses growing further out. On the far side of the pond is a large fire pit and log seating area where one or two of the older cabins will sometimes have a campfire and teaching time.

The first trip around the pond is mild compared to the rest of our trip thus far. Grider keeps Betsy in the road, if the impression of two tire tracks in the middle of a sea of grass can be called a road. He doesn't say much. He's studying the pond.

Swarms of grasshoppers fly up and land on the windshield.

"I'm ready for capture the flag!" Mark yells.

"Yeah," several others give their assent.

Maybe this is actually about to be over.

Grider guns the accelerator. We speed around the pond a second time, at least twice as fast as the first. Grasshoppers and cactus jettison in all directions. The wheels actually spin on the grass in a couple of places. How much would it take to flip Betsy?

Kids yell their wild approval. Great, he doesn't need any more encouragement.

Betsy finishes the second circuit around the pond. Grider looks back to the pond, appraising, then points the wheels toward the water and stops. What the heck is he thinking?

"Who thinks Betsy can make it through the pond!" he shouts. "Should I go?"

"Go! Go! Go! Go!" a chant starts from the kids.

Ben pumps his fist above his head and joins in. "Go! Go! Go! Go!"

There's no way the van will make it through that muck. I walked down there earlier in the summer and couldn't even make it ten feet from the water before I started sinking.

"No! No! No! No!" I yell, but am drowned out by the delirious screams of the kids and Ben. I have no idea what precedence anyone has to think that a van, even a van of Betsy's prowess, can make it through that. I'd bet against a tractor making it.

"Go Betsy!" Grider yells. He slams the gas pedal to the floor.

Betsy surges forward.

We go down a little embankment and plow through the waist-high grass. We're going about twenty miles per hour when we hit the ring of dirt around the water.

Betsy slows.

"Go!" Grider shouts. I hear the back wheels spinning.

Betsy's front end dips followed by a loud sucking sound. We come to an abrupt stop.

Can't say I didn't see this coming. I figured we'd at least make it to the water, but I can see the edge of the water out the front windshield a few feet away. That's a strange angle.

Everyone appears to be okay. The kids are laughing. Grider has his head on the steering wheel. Ben chuckles to himself under his breath.

The sucking sound again and Betsy's front end sinks several inches.

"We're going under!" Mark shouts.

"Quicksand!" someone else yells.

Surely Betsy can't sink much further, but something instinctual inside me moves. I unbuckle and throw open the door. "Come on, get out!"

The ground by the side door looks dry, but Betsy's sunk to her undercarriage so I'm not so sure. I test it with my foot and sink a couple of inches. I have fourteen kids to evacuate, so I step all the way off and sink another couple of inches. So much for my white shoes. "Go that way," I say to Mark and point to the running board on the side of the van.

Mark catches my meaning and follows the running board to the back wheels where he jumps off and scampers up to some grass on the pond embankment. The other kids follow, streaming out of the van, moving faster than I've ever seen them move before.

Ben opens his door. The bottom of it clears the mud by only a couple of inches. He steps out and sinks to his ankles. When he tries to step toward me, his foot doesn't move. He laughs to himself, and pulls hard on his leg. His foot escapes from his shoe and he pitches forward catching himself by putting his hands into the muck.

I turn away so he won't see me laugh and walk up the bank to where the kids wait. They're reliving the ride.

"Did you see that cactus blow up?" says Mark.

"Yeah, and we ran over those trees," Mason adds.

What are their parents going to think when they hear about this? I shake my head and turn back to survey the damage.

Betsy almost looks like one of those buried Cadillacs you see on postcards. Her front end is buried up to her headlights in stinky, black muck. The bumper and most of her front tires are under. The back tires are free, but a lot of good that will do. There's no way we're getting her out of there without some serious tow power.

Ben twists around, pulling on his trapped shoe. He starts to lose his balance and windmills his arms in circles to stay upright. It doesn't work and he goes down, knee and forearm in the mud.

Grider trudges up the bank, head down, black mud covering his legs halfway to his knees.

"Somebody's got to go get help," I say. I put an emphasis on the *somebody,* because it's not going to be me. I'm not telling Johnny about this.

"Yep," Grider mumbles under his breath. He doesn't look me in the eye or stop but instead walks all the way up the embankment past me and the kids. He turns toward camp on the road. What's he going to say? The mile-long trip back to camp will probably be the longest he's ever walked.

"Help."

I turn back to Betsy.

Ben is still struggling in the mud. He's got his shoe out, but has black muck on his arms, legs, and streaked on his face. It appears his second shoe is stuck. He looks like he's in the middle of a solitary game of Twister gone awry.

"Just a second." I run partway around the pond to the fire-pit. Stacked on one side are a pile of wood and a haphazard mound of limbs and kindling. I find a six-foot stick and run back.

I stretch out the stick and tiptoe to Ben. He grabs it and after lots of pulling gets himself free.

"Who wants to play Capture the Flag?" I say.

The kids cheer and run to get the flags stored under the rifle range awning. A minute later they sprint off to begin the game.

Ben and I stare at Betsy. Of all the things that have happened over the past three summers, this is the craziest. And that's saying a lot.

"Betsy, you were a good van," Ben says as if speaking a eulogy. He bows his head. "You conquered rocks, cactus, trees, cross-ties, old ladies, and tennis balls. But even Superman has kryptonite. We'll miss you, Betsy. You were almost invincible."

Several hours later Ben and I sit on the big tree swing out in front of camp.

Johnny paces in front of us. "What happened today—you know how serious it was, don't you?" He doesn't seem too upset, but has a tired, resigned look on his face. That resignation makes me more worried.

Ben and I nod.

76

"Dan told me that it was entirely his fault. He's already received his punishment. But I can't decide what to do for you. You were there. Could you have done anything to stop him?" He sighs. "I don't know."

I unclench a fist. It doesn't sound like we're getting fired.

Johnny sits between us and puts an arm around each of us. "Can you tell me what happened?"

I look across to Ben and then to Johnny. "It started with a choice..."

Richard Wines

Special Thanks

Literati, Thanks for your help editing. I like to think of us as the *Magnificent Seven*. Perhaps one day our group will be legendary.

My wonderful wife, Thanks for putting up with the quirky ways of a writer and all the late nights. I'd be completely lost without you.

Chris Ray, Thanks for your help reading this aloud and for your help with many of the facts, names, and other details.

Jen Adams, Thanks for helping with the cover photo and being my camp contact during the editing process.

Fellow T Bar M coaches, Thanks for making my time at T Bar M special. Thanks for taking me in as one of your own and for helping me live some of the best days of my life. This book is for you.

Johnny Polk, What else can I say? Hopefully this book gives some insight into who you are for those who don't know. You might be the *most interesting man in the world.*

For calling me from my everyday life and for leading me into the *Christ Centered Adventure,* I thank My Lord and Savior, Jesus Christ. I am still humbled that You considered me worthy of the title, "T Bar M Coach." None of this means anything without You. To You be the Glory.

Richard Wines

In this picture of the 1995 Staff, Richie "Leroy" Wines is the fifth Coach from the right on the front row.

29716717R00052

Made in the USA
Charleston, SC
20 May 2014